Other PaperStars by Jean Fritz

AROUND THE WORLD IN A HUNDRED YEARS
BULLY FOR YOU, TEDDY ROOSEVELT!
MAKE WAY FOR SAM HOUSTON
STONEWALL
THE GREAT LITTLE MADISON
TRAITOR: The Case of Benedict Arnold
YOU WANT WOMEN TO VOTE, LIZZIE STANTON?

JEAN FRITZ

Harriet Beecher Stowe
— AND —
THE BEECHER PREACHERS

illustrated with photographs

Penguin Putnam Books for Young Readers

PHOTOGRAPH CREDITS

Crusader in Crinoline by Forrest Wilson (Lippincott, 1941) .... pp. 34, 37, 111, 118
The Hall of Fame of Great Americans, Bronx Community College .... frontispiece
Keystone Press .... p. 95 (left)
New York Public Library Picture Collection .... pp. 47, 54, 83, 95 (right), 96
The Schlesinger Library, Radcliffe College .... pp. 49, 124
Stowe-Day Foundation, Hartford, CT .... pp. 9, 13, 15, 20, 23, 28, 40, 41, 52,
58, 60, 62, 68, 71, 74, 81, 84, 88, 92, 99, 102, 108, 114, 115, 117, 120, 122, 125, 129, 130

Copyright © 1994 by Jean Fritz. All rights reserved. This book, or parts
thereof, may not be reproduced in any form without permission in writing
from the publisher. A PaperStar Book, published in 1998 by Penguin Putnam
Books for Young Readers, 345 Hudson Street, New York, NY 10014.
PaperStar is a registered trademark of The Putnam Berkley Group, Inc.
The PaperStar logo is a trademark of The Putnam Berkley Group, Inc.
Originally published in 1994 by G. P. Putnam's Sons.
Published simultaneously in Canada. Printed in the United States of America.
Book designed by Songhee Kim. Text set in Times Roman.
Library of Congress Cataloging-in-Publication Data
Fritz, Jean. Harriet Beecher Stowe and the Beecher preachers / Jean Fritz.
p.   cm.   1. Stowe, Harriet Beecher, 1811-1896—Family—Juvenile literature.
2. Women authors, American—19th century—Biography—Juvenile literature.
3. Congregational churches—Clergy—Biography—Juvenile literature.
4. Abolitionists—United States—Biography—Juvenile literature. 5. Clergy—
United States—Biography—Juvenile literature. 6. Beecher family—Juvenile
literature. [1. Stowe, Harriet Beecher, 1811-1896. 2. Authors, American.
3. Women—Biography. 4. Abolitionists. 5. Beecher family.]   I. Title.
PS2956.F75   1994   813´.3—dc20   93-6408   CIP   AC   [B]
ISBN 0-698-11660-7
10   9   8   7   6   5   4   3   2   1

For Refna

For a careful reading of this manuscript, I am indebted to Dr. E. Bruce Kirkham of Ball State University, Muncie, Indiana, and to Suzanne Zack of the Stowe-Day Foundation in Hartford, Connecticut.

BEECHER STOWE FAMILY

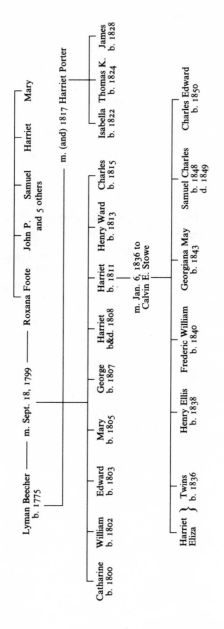

Lyman Beecher
b. 1775 — m. Sept. 18, 1799 — Roxana Foote

John P.   Samuel   Harriet   Mary
and 5 others

m. (and) 1817 Harriet Porter

Catharine
b. 1800

William
b. 1802

Edward
b. 1803

Mary
b. 1805

George
b. 1807

Harriet
b&d. 1808

Harriet
b. 1811

Henry Ward
b. 1813

Charles
b. 1815

Isabella
b. 1822

Thomas K.
b. 1824

James
b. 1828

m. Jan. 6, 1836 to
Calvin E. Stowe

Harriet }
Eliza   } Twins
b. 1836

Henry Ellis
b. 1838

Frederic William
b. 1840

Georgiana May
b. 1843

Samuel Charles
b. 1848
d. 1849

Charles Edward
b. 1850

CHAPTER ONE

Harriet Beecher had always understood that, along with her sisters, she was second best in her family. On June 14, 1811, when she'd been born, her father had grumbled to a neighbor, "Wisht it had been a boy!" Of course her father was disappointed. He was Lyman Beecher, a minister in Litchfield, Connecticut, and he was collecting boys. He wanted lots of Beecher preachers in the family. He already had three sons—William, Edward, and George—and soon there would be Henry Ward and Charles. There were also two other girls—Catharine, the oldest of them all, and Mary—and though he loved his girls dearly, their future was limited. None of them could ever stand up in public and wrestle with evil. Indeed, they would never be able to stand up in public at all. Not even to lead a prayer in church. Any woman who would try such a thing, Lyman Beecher said, "would lose the female delicacy which is above all price."

When Harriet was a girl, however, what she wanted was her father's attention, but this was hard to get. Still, she tried. Whenever the family went outdoors to pick apples or gather nuts or pile up logs, Harriet worked harder and longer than the rest, hoping that her father would notice. Sometimes he did. He might even give her the compliment she treasured most: "You would have made the best boy of the lot." Once, when she was twelve, she wrote an essay at school that was read aloud at a public meeting. Her father was so proud, he said he'd have given a hundred dollars if she had been a boy. That was the happiest moment of her childhood, she said.

To receive a compliment from Lyman Beecher was no small thing, especially for a little girl who was the sixth child in the family. Lyman Beecher was a fiery man, famous for his fiery sermons, which were supposed not only to inspire his congregation but to shake the daylights out of them. He bragged that when he stepped into the pulpit on a Sunday morning, he took hold "without mittens." He "scorched" his congregation, he said; he "switched" them; he "stamped" on them. How else could he make them repent their sins? How else could he hope that they would all get into Heaven? Of course he expected the most from his children, and they did their best. After all, they adored him.

The whole household revolved around Lyman Beecher. "Where's my hat?" he would shout. And off the children would scurry to look for Pa's hat. Or if he had a stomachache, the children knew that the next minute he'd likely take to his bed. He was not long for this world, he would moan. He must have cancer. Actually, Lyman Beecher was going into one of his fits of depression, his "hypos," the family called them— short for "hypochondria." Once he suffered such a severe hypo that he lost his voice for several months. He went to Niagara Falls, hoping to be cured. Then to Maine. Nothing worked. A doctor suggested that he try hard labor, so he plowed a neighbor's field. By the time the field was finished, his voice was strong again, and he went back to his Sunday

Lyman Beecher House, Litchfield, CT

scorchings. But a few years later he moved to Boston, and of course there were no fields to plow. So he filled half his basement with sand and worked off his hypos by shoveling sand back and forth from one side of the basement to the other.

Sometimes Lyman would simply want to have fun. He'd start a tune on his fiddle, which was a signal for a family sing. Or he'd tell stories about when he was a boy. Or he'd think of a prank to play. (He liked practical jokes.) Once he swung Catharine out of an upstairs window to see if she was brave. (She was.) But if he suddenly ran outside to break a stick off the quince tree in the front yard, the children knew there was trouble. One of them had not jumped fast enough to obey Lyman Beecher and was in for a switching. Henry Ward said he didn't mind a switching if he had his clothes on. What he hated was one the first thing in the morning before he was dressed.

It was not easy being a Beecher. Harriet would lie awake at night, listening to the wind whistling down the chimneys and the rats scratching in the walls, and she would worry. (The

Beechers could never get rid of those rats.) Her father wanted her to think about her sins, and she tried, but she couldn't seem to concentrate on them. And how could she think about anything as far away as Heaven when she couldn't even imagine what it was like to be a grown-up? As a woman, she would either be a wife or a teacher or just a plain spinster. She'd have to be submissive. Indeed, her father made clear what kind of person she *ought* to be. He knew what everyone *ought* to be, and he made no bones about it.

But what about her *feelings?* She remembered one Fourth of July when the Declaration of Independence was read aloud at a public celebration. How her heart had swelled with the full idea of independence! Suddenly she "longed to do something," she said. "I know not what: to fight for my country or to make some declaration on my own account." Sometimes she secretly thought that there might be poems inside her, but if she went dreamy, Henry Ward would laugh. "Harriet is 'owling about' again," he would say. But Catharine, who was eleven years older and bossy, would tell her to pay attention.

Harriet always said that she would have been a different person if her mother had lived. But her mother died when Harriet was not quite five years old, and two years later a stepmother took over the Beecher household. Late one night the children heard their father come home from a trip to Boston. "Here's Pa," the children cried as they jumped out of bed. Then another voice spoke up. "And here's Ma," it said. The children ran to meet her, but this new stepmother didn't look one bit like a ma. She was so beautiful, so proper-looking, she didn't seem like a person who would want to hold anyone on her lap. Indeed, "she was so elegant," Harriet said, "that we were almost afraid to go near her. I used to feel breezy and rough and rude in her presence." But the new Mrs. Beecher did know precisely how to run a house. A place for everything and everything in its place. She was a dutiful mother, and before long she had added three more children to the Beecher family. Isabella arrived when Harriet was eleven years old and later there would be Thomas and James, two more for Lyman's collection of boys.

Although the Beechers were a large family, they were not just *any* large American family. They were the *Beechers,* a special breed that would hold a unique place in America. Each of them felt the solidarity of their family, yet individually they were for the most part lonely, unhappy, often frightened children. Henry Ward said he had been starved for a kind of love that his father had been too busy to give him and his step-mother was too cold to offer. For friendship they drew on one another. Harriet was especially close to George, the brother just older than she was, and Henry Ward, the brother just younger. Harriet and George loved to garden together, plant-ing seeds and wandering in the fields to pick wildflowers. Henry Ward and Harriet shared a love of storms. At the first rumble of thunder, they would run outside, hand in hand, or just stand on the doorstep, watching the lightning rip across the sky, holding their breath in wonder. And of course the children had the Beecher dog, Trip, to play with. All her life Harriet would have a dog.

As the younger Beechers arrived, the older ones began to leave. In 1818 Edward entered Yale, and Catharine left home. She had planned on being a wife but the man she was going to marry was drowned at sea before the wedding, so now she was on her own. Like all the Beechers, she enjoyed telling people what to do, but since she couldn't preach, she would teach. "There was no usefulness for a single woman," she said, "except in a schoolroom." Still, she wouldn't be an ordinary teacher, going about teaching as if it were drudgery. She persuaded herself that women had a special mission, perhaps even more important than men. If educated properly, women, as mothers and teachers, could be the true ministers to the world. She would start a school of her own, and if her idea spread, who knew what might come of it? In 1823 she went to Hartford and opened the Hartford Female Seminary, with Mary coming along to help her teach. Although the first year there were only seven pupils, the next year there were twenty-five.

And Harriet was one of them. Catharine had found a private home where Harriet could board. Here for the first time in her life Harriet had a room of her own. It was a small, neat, cozy hall bedroom and Harriet loved it. Until she saw it, she had not realized how much she needed peace and privacy, away from the cross current of a busy family. With no one to tell her what to do, what not to do, or what kind of person she should be, she could just be herself. She could draw and paint to her heart's content—something she and Catharine both did well. There might even be space for some of those secret poems to come out.

And better yet, for the first time in her life Harriet had a friend of her own. Although she had known other girls her age in Litchfield, she hadn't been close to any of them. But at school Harriet and Georgiana May found each other almost immediately. They talked endlessly, shared private jokes, gossiped about other students, and confided secret thoughts to each other. Sometimes they took walks, exploring the city. Harriet's favorite place was a pretty little hill near the Park River. This was where she'd like to build her house someday,

Hartford Female Seminary, Hartford, CT

she said. She planned just how it would look, how many gables it would have, where her bedroom would be, where the gardens would be placed.

One day when she left Georgiana and went back to her room, she took out a new notebook filled with clean, blank pages. And she began to write a poem in it. It was a long, romantic poem about the troubles of a handsome Christian in the court of the Roman tyrant Nero. She called it "Cleon." Of course, it wasn't as good a poem as those her own hero, Lord Byron, wrote, but she had Lord Byron in mind when she described Cleon. As she added to it the poem grew from one notebook to another, as if she could not contain her dreams once she let them loose. At the same time she had to work hard on her schoolwork. Catharine was pushing her ahead as fast as she could so the next year she could also help with the teaching. Harriet was taking all the regular courses the school offered plus advanced Latin. In addition Catharine had hired a special tutor to teach her Italian and French. Catharine realized that this was a heavy load, and occasionally she would drop in to see how Harriet was doing. Once when Catharine did this, she found the notebooks. She didn't need to read much. Right away she said this was nonsense. Worthless. A waste of time. If Harriet had so little to do, Catharine said, she should begin a study of a difficult book called *The Analogy of Religion.* Next year she could teach it.

Harriet did as she was told. The next year, at fourteen, she did indeed teach the book to girls who were the same age as she was. And now she had moved from her private room to a house that Catharine had rented for the Hartford contingent of the Beecher family—Mary and Henry Ward, who was attending Catharine's school, the only boy among forty girls. But Harriet was depressed. Nor was it a temporary hypo. If sometimes her unhappiness lessened, it was never gone for long. On and on it went throughout her teenage years. At sixteen she taught two courses; at eighteen she was teaching full-time. Perhaps her depression began when she was pushed into being an adult before she was ready. When she first went to Hartford, she knew that Catharine planned for her to be a teacher and that she had nothing to say about it. Still, what else could she be? She had never expected to be anyone's wife. She was shy and short (five feet at her tallest), and she considered herself plain. So what did she expect? Why did she feel so helpless, so trapped? Her stepmother called her a "strange, inconsistent being," and that's what she was. She blamed no one but herself.

"I do nothing right," she said. "My sins take away my happiness."

"Snowy Owl" by Harriet Beecher Stowe

She was a trouble to everyone, she told Catharine. "You don't know how perfectly wretched I often feel: so useless, so weak, so destitute of all energy." Once she expressed the wish that she might die young.

Most often it was to her brother, George, studying to be a preacher, that she poured out her feelings. She was nineteen when she complained that she had to force herself to "march through slop and wet up and down main street . . . debating every step I take whether I had better lift my foot again." She felt like giving up but immediately was ashamed of that thought. "I hate myself," she said.

Yet she had the reforming spirit common to all the Beechers. She could scarcely finish a letter without offering advice. George should vary his style when he gave a sermon, she said. "Do you think ministers are apt to forget these things?" Then quickly she added, "You see that I was made for a preacher—indeed I can scarcely keep my letters from turning into sermons." Perhaps she could preach on paper, she suggested, as her brothers used their voices to preach.

But now the country itself took a hand in determining the future of Harriet Beecher. The West was opening up, and clearly the character of the United States would be affected. Lyman's scorching blood rose. He wanted a share in shaping the West. "The moral destiny of our nation," he said, "turns on the character of the West." There were plenty of people who wanted to conquer the West, but there was only one Lyman Beecher. And he wanted to conquer it for God and John Calvin. So when he was asked to be president of Lane Theological Seminary, which was opening in Cincinnati, he accepted with alacrity. And in 1832 the Beechers (all who were not working or studying elsewhere) set out on Lyman's crusade: Mrs. Beecher, Catharine (who had decided that teaching in Hartford was drudgery, after all), Aunt Esther (Lyman's half sister), George, Isabella, Thomas, four-year-old James—and Harriet.

CHAPTER TWO

Perhaps because she had none of the ambition or restlessness of the other children, Mary was the first to settle down into adulthood. In 1827 she married a young Hartford lawyer, Thomas Clapp Perkins, and came closer than any of the others to living happily ever afterward.

The boys were another story. Lyman Beecher found that once he had collected boys, it wasn't always easy to turn them into preachers. Edward, the second son, was the serious-minded one and was no trouble. He did what was expected of him, became a minister, and then went to Illinois to become president of a college. But William, the oldest son, was a problem. Indeed, it was hard for anyone to believe in him, since he had so little faith in himself. He had never learned to study and doubted if he could learn, so he saw no point in going to college.

Lyman encouraged him to start out as a cabinetmaker, but when he tried this, he didn't like it. Nor did he like clerking. After serving as a clerk in three different stores, he quit them all. Every time he came home, the family was in despair. "What shall we do with William?" they asked one another. Lyman must have put pressure on William and perhaps reminded him that his mother's dying wish was that all her sons become preachers. In any case, William finally gave in. He'd be a minister. Even though William hadn't been to college, Lyman arranged for a Boston committee to grant him a license. And in this roundabout way another son was brought into the fold. Yet, as it turned out, William wasn't much of a success as a minister either, and after two churches dismissed him, he went back home to ask his father to help him find another.

George, who was committed to the ministry, started his studies at Yale and planned to complete them at his father's new seminary. But Henry Ward was a rebel. He wanted to go to sea, but his father persuaded him to enter Amherst first. And there a lucky thing happened. He became involved in debating and discovered that there was nothing that he liked better than to stand up and address an audience. People said he was an irresistible speaker. Indeed, he sounded like his father and might even grow up to be a mite better. Henry thrived on praise, so he jumped at the chance to receive more. He'd be a preacher too. Now there was only Charles to hear from, but as the Beechers headed west, Charles was just a sophomore at Bowdoin College.

Lyman felt his family was in pretty good order. Now to convert the West! The Beechers were in high spirits as they left for Cincinnati on October 6, 1832, except for Aunt Esther and Mrs. Beecher. They would have preferred staying in New England. Not Harriet. She was ready for a new life. She was sick of familiar scenes, the same faces, the old duties, and longed for surprise to overtake her. Since she was entering a new world, she decided to make herself over too. She was twenty-one years old and she was going to quit being wretched. She had lived tight inside herself entirely too long. Her friends told her she was unsocial and she agreed. Well, that was over. From now on, instead of "shrinking into a corner," afraid of what people would think of her, she would step up to strangers, smile, and hold out her hand.

Harriet had plenty of opportunity to practice her social graces on the way west. The family took its time traveling, staying overnight with church people, visiting, and doing business on the way. Lyman was "in his element," Harriet wrote from New York, raising money for the seminary, preaching, "going here, there, and everywhere." And incidentally, he had hired a professor of Biblical literature for Lane. A man by the name of Calvin Stowe. As for herself, she was in a state of "agreeable delirium," but she admitted it was a "scattering" experience since she was always rushing about with no quiet time to think.

The trip took longer than they had expected—forty days—but if there were complaints, Harriet made light of them. They sang on the way. George and the younger children distributed religious leaflets as they went, "peppering the land," as Harriet said. Indeed, Harriet thought the Beechers must have been an amusing sight. "Here we all are," she wrote in Pennsylvania, "Noah, and his wife, and his sons and his daughters, with the cattle and creeping things, all dropped down in the front parlour of this tavern." The Beechers had no cattle or any other kind of animal with them, but Harriet liked to paint a lively picture, and she knew how to do it.

Cincinnati may have been a pleasant surprise to Mrs. Beecher and Aunt Esther, who expected any place in the west to be rough and uncivilized. The broad avenue along Cincinnati's waterfront was impressive; the houses were built of brick; and from the shoulders of the city, church spires rose just as they did in New England. At the edge of the city, columns of towering beech trees ran up Walnut Hills, the site of Lane Seminary and of the Beecher house, which was even now being built. With a new house to look forward to, they could joke about the one they were renting temporarily. It was, in Harriet's words, "the most inconvenient, ill-arranged, altogether to be execrated affair that was ever put together." Their landlord was an old bachelor, Harriet said. Only a bachelor would build a house where it was necessary to put on a coat to go to the kitchen because it was in a separate building outside.

Meanwhile the Beechers were being entertained by Cincinnati society, which was falling over itself with pride at having

Lyman Beecher House, Walnut Hills, Cincinnati, OH

lured this famous family into their midst. Lyman Beecher was the most celebrated preacher in America and, as people often said, he was "the most quoted American, except Benjamin Franklin." So with all this attention, the Beechers decided that Cincinnati was indeed an agreeable place. Except for the pigs. Mrs. Beecher objected to the pigs that roamed freely through the town. But the pigs were what four-year-old James liked best. Often he could be seen strolling down the street between two pigs, an arm around each.

Catharine, however, had no notion of letting her father win the West all by himself. Already she was planning to open a school, one that would be a model for the West. But this time she would not be bothered with teaching. She would only supervise. At first she indicated that Harriet would not be directly involved in teaching either, but in the spring of 1833, when the school opened, there was Harriet back in the same routine she had known so well in Hartford. Indeed, she was squeezing the life right out of herself—following schedules, listening to recitations, setting up rules for discipline. Day after day. There was no time left for herself. No time left for *feeling.* Of course women in America weren't supposed to have feelings of their own. And if they did, they were expected to stamp them out before they took fire. Harriet had tried stamping, she said, but her feelings burned "inward" until they burned "the very soul."

Catharine, who acted as if she were in charge of Harriet's life, could always find plenty for her to do. The summer before coming west, she persuaded Harriet to write a geography book and she arranged for its sale. She indicated that she and Harriet were joint authors, and because Catharine was better known in educational circles, she put her name first. Harriet may not have minded. She was not comfortable with public attention. Besides, even though her geography sold well, she was probably not impressed. A textbook was not her idea of writing. And teaching was not her idea of life.

While Harriet struggled against the monotony of the schoolroom, she did have several diversions. For one thing, she made a friend. Eliza, the wife of Calvin Stowe, the new professor of Biblical literature, was, like Georgiana, the kind of person she could talk to. She found Eliza's husband, however, a rather curious fellow—a short, homely, but obviously brilliant man with a countrified air about him like an old-time New Englander in baggy trousers. Harriet felt at home in their company, and when the three of them, along with Catharine, were invited to join a newly formed social group, the Semi Colon Club, Harriet accepted. The club met every other week for discussion, poetry reading, music, and refreshments, but most interesting to Harriet was the fact that they were all encouraged to write compositions to be submitted anonymously and read aloud in the group. Harriet was not ready to look into her "very soul," so she decided to try her hand at satire. She began by imitating the style of certain well-known writers, including Bishop Joseph Butler, author of *The Analogy of Religion,* which Catharine had forced her to read in Hartford. She wrote what was purported to be a letter from him, using, as she said, "his outrageous style of parenthesis and foggification." The editor of the *Western Monthly,* who was a member of the club, liked it so much he wanted to print it, but Harriet was too shy and would not give him permission to use her name. Instead, it appeared under Catharine's name.

Harriet was finding that writing for the club was *fun.* She even played a joke on the club by submitting what was sup-

Calvin Ellis Stowe

posed to be an old letter that had fallen into her hands. To make it look yellow, she smoked it; she tore it to make it look old; she sealed it and broke the seal to make it seem real. She wrote Georgiana about it. "The deception took," she said. It was lucky that it did, for if anyone had been critical, Harriet didn't know how she could have borne it. She was used to criticism within the family but not from outside.

Becoming more confident, Harriet decided to enter a short-story contest run by the *Western Monthly*. For subject matter, she drew from her memory, perhaps not even aware what a gathering kind of memory she had. Everything she had heard, seen, felt all her life was collected there in a mental album of vivid pictures. People she'd never known were all stored away. Her father's Uncle Lot, for instance, whom he used to talk about. She felt she knew Uncle Lot down to every detail of how he looked and talked and acted. So she wrote a story about him and called it "A New England Sketch." She won the first prize—fifty dollars—and when in April 1834 the story was printed, her own name was signed to it. She was twenty-two years old and that fifty dollars was like a down payment on her future. Quickly, she wrote another story, which she called "Aunt Mary." This too was published, and she had private plans for something even more ambitious—a whole book about a New England character. Her spirits were high as she confided her idea to George. He was now a minister in Batavia, Ohio, and was the one with whom she most often shared her secrets. "I love you, little Gordie," she wrote, using his childhood name. "It's a solemn fact—I believe you are the next best thing to an oyster supper and a chicken."

She had many reasons for feeling lighthearted. Summer was coming on and she'd be through with school for a while. Better yet, she'd be escaping the Cincinnati summer, which was generally an ordeal—not only because of the heat but because summer so often brought cholera epidemics to the city. But this year Harriet was going east to visit her sister Mary and Georgiana and attend Henry Ward's graduation from Amherst College. She would be making the trip with

Mary Dutton, a teacher in Catharine's school—by stage-coach to Toledo, then by steamer to Buffalo, and finally another stagecoach to Albany and from there to Massachusetts.

The trip itself turned out to be a highlight for Harriet. She had always been a people watcher, so of course travel gave her the opportunity to collect new characters and pictures for her mental album. Among her fellow passengers on the stage-coach was a "portly, rosy Mr. Smith," "a New Orleans girl looking like distraction, as far as dress is concerned," and "Miss B., a do-as-I-please sort of body." But when Harriet reached Buffalo, she forgot about the people. There was Niagara Falls! It was the most famous sight in the United States, one that even Europeans raved about, so of course Harriet was excited. Still, she wasn't prepared for it. Perhaps no one could be. "I have seen it," she wrote home, "and yet live. . . . It is not *like* anything; it did not look like anything I expected; it did not look like a waterfall. . . . Oh, it is lovelier than it is great; it is like the Mind that made it: great but so veiled in beauty that we gaze without terror. I felt as if I could have *gone over* with the waters; it would be so beautiful a death."

When after a happy summer Harriet returned to Cincinnati, Henry Ward was with her, ready to enter Lane. Charles, who had developed a passion for music, came as well. He had not graduated from Bowdoin, but he could not bear to be the only Beecher, except Mary, left in the East, so his father said he could go to Lane too. Indeed there was only one thing that marred the summer for Harriet. She received the news that Eliza Stowe had died on August 6 of cholera. Sad as Harriet was, she could only imagine Calvin's devastation. When anything went wrong in Calvin's life, he acted as if it were the end of the world. All the Beechers suffered from "hypos" from time to time, but theirs were nothing compared with Calvin's. She had watched Eliza try to coax him out of his melancholy moods, and it was hard to think of Calvin now without his Eliza.

And indeed Calvin was having a hard time. Back in Cincinnati, Harriet read the obituary he had written for Eliza. He not only described Eliza's virtues in the glowing terms commonly used at that time but he also paraded his own grief. He "wept aloud," he wrote. He still wept. The best thing for Calvin was to keep busy, and fortunately he had committed himself to giving a series of lectures that winter. Harriet was asked to report on each of them in the *Journal,* a local paper. Since the subjects were difficult and she wanted to be accurate, it was necessary for her to consult frequently with Calvin. She must also have used these sessions to bolster his spirits and keep him working. Calvin was a lifelong procrastinator who at times could only be called lazy.

In any case, over the next year Harriet came to know many sides of Calvin, but she was surprised one evening at the Semi Colon Club when he told about his visions. Ever since he'd been four years old, people had suddenly appeared before him as visions, even in the daytime. They were so clear, they didn't seem like visions, even though they were invisible to others. His favorite was a pleasant-faced man who would often look in on him after he'd gone to bed. Calvin called him Harvey and welcomed him when he came. Some were more otherworldly, like the dark-blue ghost with brown spots. Then there were the six-inch-tall white-robed fairies who jumped off the windowsill and danced around him. For a long time Calvin believed everyone had such visions, but when he realized that only he seemed to attract them, he did not worry. Nor did he try to explain. He spoke in a matter-of-fact way, somewhat surprised at himself, because, as he said, he was not an imaginative man. Harriet was not in the least put off by any of this. She believed that supernatural visits were possible. Besides, this balding, farmerish professor, nine years older than she was, had revealed a childlike side that was rather endearing.

The year 1835 was a time both of separation and of coming together for the Beecher family. George was in Batavia, Ohio; William had a church in Putnam, Ohio; Edward was still in Illinois; and ever since her school had closed, Catharine had been traveling or, as she was apt to put it, she was "flitting about," enlisting interest in her ideas of women's education. Mrs. Beecher, this second wife of Lyman's, had never been close to the children of Lyman's first marriage, but when she died in July, she did break the family circle. Perhaps the children felt their father's loneliness and wanted to comfort him. In any case, they arranged a reunion for the fall. The family had never been all together. Mary, for instance, had never even seen James.

When all eleven children assembled in Cincinnati, Lyman could scarcely contain his joy. Or his pride. What a fine collection of preachers he had gathered! He was sure that Henry Ward and Charles would soon join them and then of course there would be Thomas and James. Lyman Beecher may never have realized that it might not be quite the same God that they would worship. None of the children had ever felt at home with the harsh, merciless God that Lyman had thrust upon them in their childhood, so they searched for a more sympathetic one. It was an agonizing business. At the moment, however, they were all simply Beechers, united in their

love for one another. Not even Catharine, who so often irritated her brothers and sisters with her busybody ways, interfered with their good time.

This congregation of Beechers won the full attention of the people of Cincinnati, but there at the edge of their circle was Calvin Stowe. Would he be joining them? Would he marry Catharine or Harriet? If Harriet heard this gossip, she would have smiled. She knew the answer, and in November she and Calvin became secretly engaged. Yet even as they planned their future, sometimes she asked herself: What was she doing? Here she was, changing to "nobody knows who." Still, she went ahead. The wedding took place in January 1836, with only her family present and Mary Dutton serving as the maid of honor. Just before the ceremony, she wrote to Georgiana. What did she feel?

"Nothing at all," she wrote. She didn't understand herself, since just the week before she had looked on this wedding as an "overwhelming crisis." But Harriet didn't mail this letter, and later she added a postscript. She and Calvin were sitting by the fire "as domestic as any pair of tame fowl you ever saw. . . . I am tranquil, quiet, and happy."

Again, however, Harriet put Georgiana's letter away without mailing it. A month later she finished it. Now there was more news. She and Calvin were coming east in April, and on May 1, Calvin would sail to Europe. Commissioned by the state of Ohio to make a survey of European schools, Calvin would be traveling, particularly in Germany, for perhaps as long as a year. Harriet would see him off when he sailed.

But Harriet did not go east. In March, as she was preparing for the trip, she discovered that she was pregnant and was advised not to travel. So Harriet said good-bye to Calvin in

Cincinnati and gave him a letter, which he was not supposed to open until he'd left the United States. She wouldn't be with him to see him through bad times, so she warned him: Don't give in to hypos. Don't spoil your experience. "You are going to a new scene now. I want you to take the good of it. Only think of all you expect to see!" Harriet must have stopped to picture those sights. "My dear," she added, "I wish I were a man in your place; if I wouldn't have a grand time!"

CHAPTER THREE

What was really important in Harriet's life was not just what she did but what she saw happening around her. Cincinnati may have been on the edge of the West, but it was also on the edge of the South, right across the river from Kentucky, a slave-owning state. Harriet had hated the idea of slavery ever since she'd been a little girl and Aunt Mary, her mother's sister, had run away from her husband, a planter in Jamaica, because she couldn't stand to see how his slaves were treated. For a couple of years, until she died, this sickly aunt lay in the Beecher kitchen, suspended from the ceiling in a hammock she had brought with her from Jamaica. Harriet never forgot the picture of her swaying in the midst of their housekeeping. Nor could she forget the slaves. It was as if she'd brought them right into the kitchen.

Slavery was very much on the minds of New Englanders throughout Harriet's childhood. She remembered how the tears ran down her father's face at family prayers when he got going on the subject. Yet Lyman Beecher was not an abolitionist, stirring up public opinion to abolish all slavery then and there. He did not believe that all slaves should be freed immediately. He was for a more gradual emancipation, a freeing that would not disrupt the entire society and perhaps even start a civil war. He favored the colonization idea, which would send freed slaves to Africa to establish a colony of their own. The Beecher family all supported Lyman's view. The abolitionists with their fiery talk were just making things worse, Harriet said. They were just too extreme or too "ultra," to use a slang expression that was a favorite with Harriet.

Nevertheless, what Harriet was seeing in Cincinnati filled her with anger. When she read a notice offering a reward for the capture of a runaway slave, she longed to help that runaway to freedom. Sometimes she would see a boat going down the river with a cargo of chained slaves. She knew those chained men were going South to be sold; she could even picture the auction block.

Once she and her father and Calvin had attended a church meeting in Ripley, Ohio, staying overnight at the home of the minister, John Rankin. The house sat on the top of a hill at the end of a narrow path that led to the Ohio River below. Sitting on the veranda that evening, looking down on the river and at the Kentucky shore on the other side, John Rankin told a story that Harriet would never forget. In his window stood a lighted lantern, which, Harriet learned, was a signal to runaways that this was a safe house. Once in early spring, when the river, which had been frozen, was breaking up, a young runaway woman and her baby had stepped on that crumbling ice. Stumbling, falling, wet, she had managed to cross the river and drag herself and her baby to the safety of John Rankin's house. The scene that Mr. Rankin described was as vivid to Harriet as if she'd been there, as if she herself had been the runaway.

Because Cincinnati stood at the crossroads between the

North and the South, tempers ran high, and there seemed to be no room for anyone who tried to hold the middle ground. If you weren't an abolitionist, you were accused of supporting slavery. There needed to be an "intermediate society," Harriet said, but it became increasingly hard to be intermediate. When Lyman Beecher tried to establish order in the seminary after an abolitionist student had stirred up disturbance, he was accused of running "a prison of oppression." On the other hand, pro-slavery people attacked James Birney, an abolitionist who had started a newspaper in their city.

The trouble came to a head in July 1836. Harriet was living in her father's house during Calvin's absence; Henry Ward was acting as editor of the *Journal* while the regular editor was away. A mob broke into Birney's printing establishment and damaged the press, but in spite of difficulties Mr. Birney managed to print an edition the next day. Henry Ward wrote an editorial condemning the mob, and Harriet wrote an article supporting the freedom of the press, but the mob didn't care about editorials and articles.

"For my part," Harriet wrote Calvin, "I hope he [Mr. Birney] will stand his ground. The office is fire-proof. . . . I wish he would man it with armed men and see what can be done. If I were a man, I would go, for one, and take good care of at least one window."

The mob did more damage and gave up only after the mayor of Cincinnati swore in a group of armed volunteers to defend the streets. Henry Ward was one of them. "For a day or two," Harriet reported, "we did not know but there would be war to the knife . . . and we really saw Henry depart with his pistols with daily alarm, only we were all too full of patriotism not to have sent every brother we had."

If only she had been a man! It would have been surprising

Henry Ward Beecher

if Harriet had not thought this. And equally surprising if Harriet was not quite as "intermediate" as she had once been.

Mr. Birney left town. Shortly after this, Lyman Beecher returned from Boston with his third wife, Mrs. Lydia Jackson, who was no more popular with Lyman's first seven children than his second wife had been. And on September 29, Harriet gave birth to twin daughters, Eliza and Isabella.

The twins were four months old before Calvin returned from Europe. Indeed, because his trip home was unusually stormy and long, he didn't even know he had twins. The first thing he did was to rename Isabella. If there was an Eliza named for his first wife, there should be a Harriet named for this wife. She would be called Hattie for short, like her mother.

It took a while for the Stowes to settle down as a family again. For one year Calvin had been meeting important people and seeing interesting sights, without the usual worries. And now he walked into a city torn apart by arguments over slavery. As it turned out, the problem came right into their home. Harriet had hired a young black servant girl who claimed to be free but apparently wasn't. One day the girl came home from town in a panic, confessed that she was a runaway, and said that her master had come to Cincinnati to find her. Harriet swung into action. Here was something she could *do.* That night she put the girl into the back of a covered wagon, which Calvin and Henry Ward drove twenty miles over back roads to the farm of a Mr. Van Zandt, who, like John Rankin, ran a safe house on the Underground Railroad. Calvin and Henry Ward were each armed with a pistol, and as Harriet watched them drive off, she must have felt that she was continuing the story of Mr. Rankin's runaway. Surely she took satisfaction in the knowledge that, whether she was a man or not, she had helped at least one slave to freedom.

Slavery was touching the lives of other Beechers as well. In Alton, Illinois, Edward had helped Elijah Lovejoy, the editor of another abolitionist newspaper, as he faced an armed mob. The mob had fired at Elijah. When Cincinnati first heard the news, the story was that both Elijah and Edward had been killed. A later report was more accurate. Elijah had been killed but Edward had not been present at the moment. The Beechers breathed again.

Another Beecher moved South to New Orleans into the midst of slavery. Charles had dropped out of his father's preacher collection, saying that he was not sure that he even believed in God. Lyman had no intention of giving up on Charles. Every week the whole family prayed together that Charles would see the light and be saved. In the meantime Charles was traveling the countryside, collecting debts for a cotton merchant and writing home about the people he was meeting. He told about a Yankee who had moved to Louisiana to farm. This Yankee had doubled his fist before Charles. "Well, I tell ye yer fist had got as hard as iron knocking down niggers. I never see a nigger yet I couldn't bring down in one crack."

Harriet never forgot Charles's story, but at the moment she had other things on her mind. In January 1838 Harriet gave birth to a son, Henry, so now she had three children under two years old. This in itself was a full-time job, but Harriet had to make money. Lane Seminary was limping along with few students and so little money that some months Lyman Beecher could not even pay his professors. Calvin was completely distracted. He had always lived in terror of being poor, and what lay ahead now? The poorhouse, what else? Harriet began writing again, sending out short essays to every publication she could think of. She signed her work "Mrs. Harriet E. Beecher Stowe." Fortunately, she had no trouble selling what she wrote, and with her first money she hired a German girl to do the housework. This gave her three hours to write every day, and she meant to keep on writing. "I have determined," she wrote Mary Dutton, "not to be a mere domestic

The Cincinnati that Harriet knew

slave." Moreover, she wanted to make clear that when she wrote, she did it for *pay*.

In the fall, when Lane was to open for a new semester, most of the students had withdrawn, some for financial reasons, some because the question of abolition had divided the student body. It looked as if Lane would simply have to close down. To Calvin Stowe, this was the end of the world. He went to bed. Lyman Beecher, however, thought nothing was impossible. He'd just have to scare up more students. So off he went, and when he came back, he had a dozen new students—six from Edward's college, the rest from Marietta College.

He charged into the Stowes' house. "Stowe," he cried, "I've brought you twelve students. Get up and wash, eat bread, and prepare to have a good class."

Although she needed to keep writing, Harriet could not stick to her resolution. She managed to send off a few pieces, but trying to write in her house was like raking leaves in a windstorm. She could hardly start a sentence before the children would get into a fight, the fire would need attention, or someone would be at the door. There were four children now. Fred had been born in May 1840. Often Harriet had to let the housework go as she tended to the children, but when she did she felt guilty. She knew what kind of wife and mother she *ought* to be. If she had any doubts, Catharine would enlighten her.

Catharine was writing "how to" books for women. How to cook, how to raise children, how to decorate a house, how to eat, how to dress, how to exercise, how to behave. She told women how to manage their husbands even though she herself had never had a husband. It sounded like a tricky business, since women were always supposed to be subordinate to men. Actually, Catharine didn't act subordinate to anyone. She told everyone what to do, often taking over to such an extent that her family dreaded her visits. Once, when staying with a niece, she fired the niece's maid because she wouldn't obey Catharine. A woman, even a maid, Catharine said, should "pursue a perfect standard of rectitude."

No one carried the idea of perfection higher than George. He was the most brilliant one and the one most aware of falling short of what he *ought* to be. In addition, he was pained by how much the world itself fell short. All the Beechers had "nerves," a friend once remarked, but George more than the rest. Slavery upset him so much that he became an abolitionist—the first of the Beechers to go this far. Now married and preaching in Rochester, New York, he had taken up with a religious school of thought called Perfectionism, which he tried to explain in letters to his brothers and sisters. Harriet said it was too much for her and instead asked George for advice on planting dahlias.

With George in Rochester and William in Batavia, New York, the family seemed to be slowly making its way east again. Harriet longed to go too and envied Catharine the free and easy way she went back and forth. On one of her trips to New York to see her publisher, Catharine offered to take with her some of Harriet's short stories. Perhaps her publisher would be interested in bringing out a collection of these stories in book form. Harriet gathered up her New England sketches, beginning with "Uncle Lot," but she didn't count on anything as grand as a *book*. As it turned out, however, the publisher (Harper & Brothers) was interested, and Catharine wrote that she would make the arrangements.

No! Harriet wanted to make her own arrangements. Calvin agreed. In a flurry of excitement Harriet left for New York. She went straight to the publisher's office and looked, she supposed, like any author going about her business, but she wasn't any author. This was Harriet Beecher Stowe becoming a new person. At the moment she was not a daughter or a wife or a sister or a mother. She was not just another Beecher. She was only *herself.* And she was talking about royalties. She was signing a contract. She was giving her book a name—*The May Flower.* And yes, of course there would be more books. Oh, there was no end to the possibilities!

Harriet was walking on air as she wrote to Calvin explaining the terms of the agreement. "For a second volume, I shall be able to make better terms. On the whole, my dear, if I choose to be a literary lady, I have, I think, as good a chance of making profit by it as anyone I know of."

When Calvin replied, he said exactly what Harriet needed to hear. "My dear, you must be a literary woman. It is so written in the book of fate." He told Harriet to drop the middle initial, E, from her name. "Write yourself fully and always Harriet Beecher Stowe." It sounded better.

From New York Harriet went to Hartford to visit Mary.

Title page of The May Flower, *Harriet's first book*

Letters raced back and forth between Harriet and Calvin over the next weeks, with Harriet trying out her new role and Calvin backing her up.

"If I am to write," Harriet said, "I must have a room to myself, which shall be *my* room."

Calvin agreed. "You must make all your calculations to spend the rest of your life with your pen." But Calvin missed her. "The fact is," he wrote, "I cannot live without you. There is no woman like you in this wide world."

Never had Calvin and Harriet seemed to love each other as much as they did now, when one was in Cincinnati and the other in the East. "If you were not already my dearly loved husband," Harriet wrote, "I should certainly fall in love with you."

Harriet Beecher Stowe was thirty-one years old and obviously excited by this glimpse of herself as a literary lady. The excitement, however, did not survive the trip west. Once she was back in Cincinnati, the literary lady was overwhelmed by Harriet the mother and Harriet the wife.

CHAPTER FOUR

Harriet may have fixed up a room for herself, but if so, she didn't write about it. She was writing, however—short magazine pieces scratched out in desperation to help with family expenses. Nothing worthy of a book. She hated this business of writing only when she *had* to. She hated being poor, poorer than she and Calvin had ever been. Besides, Harriet was sick most of the time. Soon after returning from New York, she became pregnant again, but this time she was having more trouble than before. Tired and discouraged, Harriet described the winter of 1842–43 as a "season of sickness and gloom."

In the spring Harriet received copies of *The May Flower.* Seeing her name on the binding of the book may have revived her ambition to be a literary lady, but it may also have depressed her. In August she would have a total of five children, and although nothing was ever as important to Harriet as her children, how could she be a literary lady too?

In July, a month before the baby was due, real tragedy struck. George died. No, it was worse than that. One morning before breakfast, seeing a flock of robins descend on his sweet-cherry tree, George took his double-barreled gun, went outside, and fired the first barrel into the tree. Then he put the muzzle of the gun into his mouth and pulled the trigger again. None of the family ever admitted that George's death was anything but an accident, but how could they understand it? How could they get used to the fact that George was *gone?* Harriet couldn't shake off the picture of George standing under his cherry tree in a flurry of frightened robins, his gun raised to his face. She *needed* George, and if the new baby was a boy, she would name him George.

George Beecher

But when the baby arrived in August, it was a girl, a very frail and fretful girl who seemed to be teetering on the edge of life. Harriet named her Georgiana May after her school friend, and although the baby did eventually grow strong, Harriet did not recover as she should. Putting Georgiana in the care of a hired nurse, Harriet dragged herself about, worrying all the time what this nurse would do next. She was not to be trusted. She had unexpected fits of temper and Harriet never knew what would set her off. For Harriet that entire year was a nightmare. It was as if the whole world were sliding from under her feet and she didn't know "where the ground would open next." Perhaps under her father, her brothers, her husband. Any or all. She was haunted by the fear that tragedy, once started, couldn't be stopped.

The only good thing that happened was that Charles was back in the fold. Harriet had written him often, describing her own religious experiences in an obvious attempt to influence him, but Charles had not appreciated her efforts. Her letters sounded "too wise," he said. They didn't sound like her; they sounded more like Catharine. In any case, he came north (with his new wife, Sarah) and went to Indianapolis to be with Henry. And there, during a revival in 1843, he admitted he came close to conversion. Henry Ward was so confident that Charles would come around that he wrote his father, "I feel that Charles is *safe.*" And from the Beecher point of view, he was. Indeed, before long he was a pastor in Fort Wayne, Indiana.

But no matter what happened, Harriet remained tied down to her children and her housework. She longed for a rest, for relief from the half-dead feeling of pushing herself through each day. But of course there was no money to do anything or go anywhere. Calvin could go to a church convention in Detroit, but Harriet could only stay home and write him letters.

"It is a dark, sloppy, rainy, muddy, disagreeable day," she wrote, "and I have been working hard (for me) all day in the kitchen, washing dishes, looking into closets, and seeing a great deal of that dark side of domestic life. . . . I am sick of the smell of sour milk, and sour meat, and sour everything, and then the clothes *will* not dry, and no wet thing does, and everything smells mouldy; and altogether I feel as if I never wanted to eat again."

In theory Harriet agreed with Catharine that there was no nobler profession than that of a housewife or homemaker. She agreed that housework should be regarded as a science that women should master, apply, and be cheerful about. Indeed at a later date she would even collaborate with Catharine on her "how to" books. But that was theory and this was now and she felt rotten. "I feel no life," she said, "no energy, no appetite, or rather a growing distaste for food." Actually, she was worried about herself. Sometimes it seemed that her brain just gave out. She went blank and couldn't think what needed to be done or remember what had been done. It was a scary feeling, far worse than just being sick or weary. Her only comfort was that Catharine had suffered nervous breakdowns but had recovered after several months of treatment at one of the popular water-cure establishments. Of course the treatment was expensive, but Harriet reasoned that if she was meant to go, she would go. If God willed it. "He can easily find means," she said. "Money, I suppose, is as plenty with Him now as it always has been."

She didn't sound hopeful, but apparently she was meant to

go. In the spring of 1846 she entered the water-cure center at Brattleboro, Vermont. All she would say was that the money had come from "unknown hands," but Catharine must have raised the money simply by asking friends for contributions. She was not shy about asking for favors. Indeed, she had financed her own treatment by persuading friends that her cure was in the interest of education.

It is hard to understand why the water cure was so popular throughout the United States. The treatment couldn't have been pleasant. Patients were wrapped mummylike in wet sheets for hours at a time. They were dunked in icy baths, filled with glass after glass of water, and doused under a pounding eighteen-foot waterfall for ten minutes each day. Harriet talked of the "tedious and wearisome baths," yet waterlogged or not, she seemed to be having a good time. Most important, she was free of responsibility. Instead of waiting on others from morning until night, she was waited upon. All her attention was centered on herself and her health, and she wasn't going to spoil it by worrying. Their nurse had calmed down, and even before Harriet left, Calvin had apparently learned to take care of the children. To Georgiana, Harriet had written: "You would laugh to see him [Calvin] gravely marching the little troop in their nightgowns up to bed, tagging after them, as he says, like an old hen after a flock of ducks."

But Calvin often felt sorry for himself. Here he was, he sighed, feeling poorly, abandoned to a life of domestic disorder. Calvin couldn't stand anything out of place. He objected to furniture being rearranged. He hated to see a newspaper scattered helter-skelter on the floor. Perhaps the maid had been careless with Calvin's newspaper, but Harriet, a

*Forms of therapeutic bathing as practiced
in the nineteenth century*

longtime newspaper dropper, was used to this complaint. She replied lightly, "I really pity you in having such a wife."

In letter after letter Calvin grumbled about his health. He'd feel better, Harriet told him, if he'd only *amuse* himself. Why didn't he learn to dance? Since the Beechers didn't approve of dancing, Harriet must have felt mischievous. Besides, the picture of her goblinlike husband on a dance floor so delighted her that she went on. Why not teach her mother and father too? And some of the prim ladies from church. They could all go together to dancing cotillions!

Harriet had no trouble amusing herself. It was as if she were making up for the fun she'd missed while growing up. "I wish you could be with me in Brattleboro," she wrote, "and coast down hill on a sled, go sliding and snowballing by moonlight! I would snowball every bit of the *hypo* out of you!"

When Harriet returned to Cincinnati in late spring 1847, she could manage the house and five children with little trouble and no complaints. A sixth child, however, would make it difficult, but in January 1848 a sixth child, Samuel Charles, arrived. Naturally a new baby in the house made for confusion and disorder, which may have increased Calvin's sense of his own poor health. In any case, he did not feel at all well, and it was decided that it was his turn to try the water cure. Lane Seminary was able to give him a leave of absence and enough money to pay for his cure but barely enough to support his family.

After Calvin left in June, Harriet took in boarders and started a small school to bring in more money. And then Catharine, the family problem solver, arrived on the scene. She knew better than to visit when Calvin was at home, for those two did not get along. But Catharine had always felt a special responsibility for Harriet, and now she had all kinds of plans for them to carry out together. Harriet wrote to Calvin about them and, as might have been expected, Calvin exploded. Oh, he knew Catharine, he said. She'd start a project and then she'd run off, leaving Harriet to carry on alone. " 'It isn't heavy,' Catharine would say, 'it isn't heavy at all, you can carry it with perfect ease.' I will have nothing to do with her in the way of business. . . . She would kill off a whole regiment like you or me in three days." Presumably Harriet did not join Catharine in her projects. Presumably Calvin cooled off in a cold bath. In any case, Harriet was soon too busy to do anything but watch over her children.

Cholera broke out in Cincinnati in 1849. Every summer there were cases here and there, but this summer it was an epidemic. On June 25, eighty-four people died. Day by day the number went up in spite of the heavy smoke that was supposed to keep the disease from spreading. Indeed, the city looked as if it were on fire, with smoke billowing up from coal fires set on every street corner. Soot from the fires fell like black snow, covering the streets, filtering through windows to lie in a film over rugs, furniture, books, everything. The air, Harriet said, seemed to "lie like lead on the brain and soul." People tried to stay indoors, peeking between lace curtains when they heard a cart lumbering past. Yes, another hearse. More coffins. On July 4 there were 1,081 burials. Who would be next? That was the question on every mind.

On July 9 the baby, whom they called Charley, took sick, but as it turned out, it wasn't cholera. On July 12, eleven-year-old Henry began vomiting, but again Harriet's family was spared. On July 16 the Stowes' dog, Daisy, had a fit and died. Then on July 19 Charley went into convulsions. The doctor said he couldn't live more than a few days.

Harriet wrote Calvin. He shouldn't come home, she said. He must not expose himself. When a few days later Charley died, Harriet managed everything by herself while mourning for "my beautiful, loving, gladsome baby, so loving, so sweet,

Samuel Charles Stowe

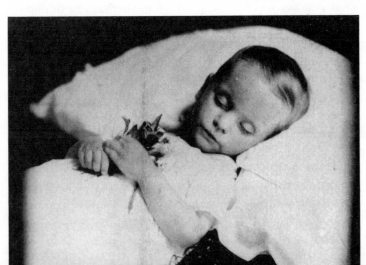

so full of life and hope and strength." It was the hardest loss she had ever had—little Charley, who had not even had a chance at life.

The year 1849 was a time when Americans were moving west, not just to Ohio and Illinois but all the way to California, where gold had been discovered. Harriet must have seen wagon trains rolling through Cincinnati. She must have watched Ohio riverboats filled with exuberant young men on the way to the goldfields. But the Beechers were going the other way. One by one they were gradually returning east. Henry Ward was already making a name for himself as pastor of the Plymouth Church in Brooklyn, New York. Thomas (twenty-four years old) was principal of a high school in Hartford, Connecticut, but he had tried many careers. He was one of the Beecher resisters. Once he had talked of going to West Point or being a Rocky Mountain trapper, but instead he had made astronomical instruments for a while, then had assisted a professor of chemistry in a medical college. In the end Lyman, as always, had his way. Thomas was not yet ordained, but he would be in 1851.

James, twenty-one years old, was another resister. When in 1848 he boarded a clipper ship for China, perhaps he thought he was going beyond the reach of his father's prayers. If so, he underestimated his father's power. He was away five years, but eventually he recognized that willy-nilly he would be a minister too. "That's my fate," he said. "Father will pray me into it."

As for Isabella, by 1849 she had been married for eight years to John Hooker in Hartford and had three children. But Isabella was a Beecher through and through. Before marrying John, a law clerk, she had persuaded him to give up law for the ministry. Indeed, she enlisted Lyman's and Catharine's help in her campaign, and under their combined pressure John did go to Yale Divinity School—briefly. Then he returned to Hartford, to law, and to Isabella, who tried to be a perfect wife and mother yet complained of the "tameness and insipidity" of her daily life.

Catharine, of course, continued to be Catharine. She was writing, traveling between the East and the West, and lecturing—but not personally taking the platform, because that would have been indelicate. When she could, she persuaded Thomas to accompany her so he could read her speeches. She always found someone to accompany her, even though women were beginning to speak in public. Indeed some women now were actually promoting woman's rights, even the right to vote. In 1848 they had held a woman's-rights convention in Seneca Falls, New York, but Catharine didn't go along with them. She held fast to what she believed was her God-given femininity and at the same time was as bossy as ever.

Of the Beecher children, only Charles was left in the West. And Harriet. She was thirty-eight years old now and had spent seventeen years in Cincinnati, and that was enough. More than enough. She longed to return to New England. She didn't know how it could be managed, but when Calvin returned in September, he had news so incredible that if Harriet didn't break into a dance, she must have felt like it. Calvin had been offered a teaching post at Bowdoin College, his alma mater, in Brunswick, Maine. But how could they afford it? he asked. Bowdoin only offered $1,000 a year, less than he'd been getting at Lane (when he'd been paid).

Oh, never mind, Harriet said. Never mind. They could manage. She would be careful. She would write. She would teach. He mustn't worry about money. Let's just go!

Calvin couldn't leave Lane until the end of the school year

in June, but Harriet went ahead. In the spring of 1850 she took three of her children with her (Hattie, fourteen years old; Fred, ten; and Georgiana, seven) and left the other two (Eliza, fourteen, and Henry, twelve) with Calvin. She wanted to make the trip and get settled in Maine before July, when another baby was due.

Although Harriet didn't realize it, her future was being decided at that very moment—not in Brunswick or in Cincinnati but in Washington, D.C., where something called the Fugitive Slave Law was being debated.

CHAPTER FIVE

The argument in Washington was—as always, it seemed—between the North and the South. California wanted to come into the Union as a free state, but Southerners insisted that another free state would make the North even more powerful than it already was. And they'd had enough of the North trying to control them, acting self-righteous, flooding them with hateful antislavery propaganda. If California became a free state, some of the Southern states threatened to secede, to leave the Union. Three of the country's greatest political statesmen were leading the debate: John C. Calhoun for the South, Daniel Webster of Massachusetts for the North, and Henry Clay, senator from Kentucky—called the Great Compromiser, because twice before he had saved the Union when it seemed on the brink of breaking up. All three men were famous orators. All three were at the end of their careers and making their last passionate plea for what they believed.

Calhoun maintained that secession could be avoided only if the South had equal rights in new territories and if the North was legally restrained from meddling in the question of slavery. Henry Clay proposed various concessions to the South, but the one to which the North objected most strenuously was

the Fugitive Slave Act. This would give the federal government not only the power but also the incentive to catch runaways and return them to their masters.

Daniel Webster had always been a hero to New Englanders.
At every opportunity he had opposed Calhoun. He had called
slavery a "great moral and political evil" and would always be
remembered for proclaiming, "Liberty *and* Union, now and
forever, one and inseparable." And what did Daniel Webster
say now? On March 7 Daniel Webster, born and bred in New
England, stood on the floor of the Senate and supported
Clay's compromise. Even the Fugitive Slave Act.

Harriet, getting ready to leave Cincinnati, reacted as many

Henry Clay

New Englanders did. She felt betrayed. This new act was not just slave owners hunting down their runaways. The Fugitive Slave Act would, in effect, make the North an accessory to slavery, cooperating in its survival, participating in the sin. All over the North, special United States commissioners would be scouting around for runaways, issuing warrants for their arrest. And moreover, they would be paid—$10 every time they returned an arrested black to his owner, $5 every time they made an arrest but couldn't deliver. In addition, this law endangered free blacks in the North. If arrested, a so-called fugitive could not speak in his own behalf, nor would he be allowed a trial by jury. And there were penalties: a $1,000 fine for any marshal refusing to make an arrest, and $1,000 for any citizen hiding a runaway or interfering in his arrest.

Reading the details of the law, Harriet was inflamed and could hardly wait to hear what her brothers had to say about it. On her way to Maine, she would be visiting both Henry Ward in Brooklyn and Edward in Boston. It was a long trip east by steamboat and train, and when she reached Brooklyn in the middle of the night, she must have been a bit over-whelmed by Henry Ward. Of course she knew he was popular, but he was *rich* too. "Henry's people are more than ever in love with him," she wrote to Calvin. They had raised his salary to $3,300 and had given him a beautiful horse and carriage costing $600. And they *should* love him, for he loved them. He wanted to be close to his congregation, so he had refused to use a pulpit. Instead he had a platform built in the midst of the people, so he would be standing in full view of them. Then he loosed the full force of his personality, the whole range of his theatrics, on his congregation—2,500 regu-larly, with visitors lined up outside to hear him. "I thought I knew how to preach," Lyman Beecher once said, "until I heard Henry."

As for slavery, Henry Ward had for a long time been hesitant to take a public stand against it. Like his father, he had opposed the extreme measures of the abolitionists and didn't want to be mixed up with them. But Henry was against Clay's compromise. In a few weeks he would go even further. "I disown the Act," he would cry.

In Boston Edward Beecher and his wife, Isabella, were so infuriated by the Act, they talked of little else. Ever since his abolitionist friend Elijah Lovejoy had been murdered in Illinois, Edward had been an avid abolitionist, befriending blacks, free and fugitive.

Harriet may have met Josiah Henson at Edward's house on this trip, or perhaps she just heard about him. In any case, she never forgot his story. As a young slave, Josiah had been beaten by a neighbor's white overseer until both shoulders had been broken. Later he made a deal with his master. If he could make $600 by working on the side for other people, he could buy his freedom. But when he came up with the money, his master told him he needed twice that amount. Then he threatened to sell Josiah. That was enough. Taking his family, Josiah escaped and made his way to Canada, where he educated himself and became a Methodist preacher. Harriet marveled at Josiah Henson. With every reason to be filled with hate, Josiah actually prayed for his former master. And to think that under the Fugitive Slave Act a man like Josiah Henson could be arrested! He would not even be permitted to tell his story.

But the Act had not become law yet. Congress would have to vote first, and that might take several months. Meanwhile

Harriet had to move her family to Brunswick, fix up a house, have a baby, and if possible, start making money. Calvin had been able to get Bowdoin to add another $500 to his salary; Harriet had borrowed $100 from George's widow. But even counting on what she might earn, she knew that they would spend more than they would make. All she could do was to keep busy, and she had no trouble doing that. Their home in Brunswick was large and handsome, one in which Longfellow had lived while a student at Bowdoin, but still there was work to be done. Walls had to be painted, windowpanes replaced, a new sink put in, sofas recovered, furniture revarnished, and bedspreads made, and in the midst of this a letter arrived from Calvin in Cincinnati. He was having a hypo. He was sick abed, he said, all but dead, and for all he knew, Harriet might soon be a widow. He warned her to be careful with money. If he died, he didn't see how she'd ever get out of debt. Harriet crushed the letter in her hand, threw it into the stove, and ran to her next chore.

Calvin (apparently none the worse for wear) arrived in Brunswick with the two other children the first week of July. On July 8, the baby, the last of the Stowe children, was born—another Charley, officially named Charles Edward. On the following day the president of the United States, Zachary Taylor, died of cholera. For a few days the newspapers were filled with details of the funeral. He hadn't been a particularly popular president, yet his funeral procession was five miles long with Whitey, his favorite horse, marching behind the hearse. But what about the Compromise of 1850? It hadn't been voted on yet. The new president, Millard Fillmore, was from New York. Would he take a strong stand on enforcing the Fugitive Slave Act if it became law?

Stowe House, Brunswick, ME

On September 12 the Fugitive Slave Act did become law. Boston fired one hundred guns to celebrate the Union's survival. There would be no war. Harriet certainly didn't want a war, but she couldn't celebrate. The Fugitive Slave Act was like a wound in her body with no prospect for healing. And Calvin would not be with her to follow events as they unfolded. Indeed, he was in a delicate position. Lane Seminary couldn't find an immediate replacement for him and claimed he was under obligation to them for the three-month winter term. At the same time he had signed a contract with Bowdoin, and now Andover Theological Seminary in Massachusetts invited him to join their faculty. The Andover position was the best opportunity he'd ever been offered, and Calvin couldn't bear to let it go. He juggled negotiations with the three institutions and finally reached an agreement—a few months here and there until 1852, when he would be free to teach full-time at Andover.

In December Calvin left for Cincinnati, leaving Harriet in a bustle of activity. Fortunately, she had more energy than she remembered ever having. She took on all the housework herself and hired a woman (perhaps a relative of Lyman's third wife) to help with the children and to teach in the little school she opened in an upstairs room of her house. Harriet herself taught the course in English history and at the request of neighbors painted or drew pictures, for which she'd always had talent. Most important, she wrote, wrote, wrote—descriptive sketches, sermonettes, humorous pieces for magazines, on subjects that were typically relegated to genteel women writers in America. She was making small sums of money, but writing, she said, was like rowing against wind and tide. She had neither quiet nor privacy. Upstairs was the

"Casco Bay" by Harriet Beecher Stowe

noise of the schoolroom, downstairs the girls each practiced on the piano two hours a day, and of course there were eternal interruptions from the children and from the chores that needed to be done.

Still, Harriet and the children managed to have fun that winter. When the snow fell, Harriet determined to revive her Brattleboro good times. She bought sleds for the children, and together they coasted down Brunswick's hills and threw snowballs. At Christmas Harriet brought a tree into the house and decorated it with painted walnut shells, pine cones, and any kind of fancy gewgaws she and the children could dream up. For Harriet, even having a tree was a small act of revolution, since her father, as one of the last real Puritans, had outlawed all recognition of Christmas, a pagan holiday that, he said, no good Christian would observe. As a child Harriet had envied the Episcopalians, who celebrated Christmas with pine boughs in their church, candles, and carols. She had crept down to the church in Litchfield, perhaps with George or Henry Ward, and peeked in at all that forbidden beauty. And now she was determined that her children were not going to miss out.

There must have been times when Harriet understood how inhibited she'd been as a child, trying to be someone she *ought* to be. She once wrote that "a man cannot ravel out the stitches in which early days have knit him," and surely it was partly because of those stitches that Harriet took on the burden of slavery as if it were her own. And the burden was heavy now. Newspapers were filled with stories of "slave-snatchers" and "man-stealers," and President Fillmore was threatening to send troops to enforce the law wherever it was needed. What made Harriet most angry, however, was that among the Boston clergy, only Edward preached against the law. The church had a specific duty, she felt, to speak out against immorality, legal or not legal. Slavery, she believed, could not survive if the entire church, both North and South, united against it.

As a Beecher, she believed firmly that *words* had the power to make changes. Her father used to say that the world might be a different place if only he'd had a chance to work on Napoleon. And now Harriet, frustrated at not being able to *do* anything herself, could only wish. If only her father could come to Boston and preach against the Fugitive Slave Act! If only another Martin Luther would rise up and set the country right! If only she were a man! Surely she would have wished this too.

Edward's wife, Isabella, wrote regularly to Harriet with the latest news from Boston. Like Harriet, Isabella was frustrated that she couldn't *do* anything, but why couldn't Harriet? "If

Harriet Beecher Stowe with her twin daughters, Eliza Tyler and Harriet Beecher Stowe

I could use a pen as you can," she wrote in one emotional letter, "I would write something that will make this whole nation feel what an accursed thing slavery is."

At a single stroke Isabella's letter filled Harriet with excitement, determination, and a sense of power. She found herself speaking aloud. "I will do it," she cried. "I will if I live."

But how? This would demand an entirely different kind of writing than she'd ever attempted. Slavery was not only a moral question, it was a political one, the province of men who dealt in propaganda. Would she seem unwomanly to be attacking such a subject? Would she embarrass her brothers? Would Calvin approve?

She was still mulling it over when Henry Ward came to visit in January after giving a speech in Boston. He arrived in the middle of the night in a raging snowstorm. Although he didn't have the strong features and good looks of his brothers, Henry Ward was a dramatic figure. The cape that he affected these days swirled around him; his stylish fedora hat was pulled down over his long, blowing hair. He'd been to Europe since Harriet had last seen him, and she would have questions about that. They talked most, however, about slavery. All night in front of the fire they talked, while Henry jiggled and rubbed the handful of uncut jewels he always carried in his pocket. The jiggling seemed to work off some of his nervous energy, and he had a lot of energy as he described what he planned to do about slavery. At last Harriet admitted that she thought she'd write something. "Do it," Henry Ward said. He had such a hearty, positive way of talking, it was impossible to believe that he could be wrong about anything. If only she could see how to go ahead!

It was over a month before Harriet came up with an idea

and then it struck out of the blue. She was sitting in church one cold Sunday in February when suddenly a picture appeared before her, almost like a vision. She could see the scene as clearly as if she had been transported to the Deep South. A slave was being beaten to death by his master with the help of two of his lackeys. In the background was a plantation on the edge of a swamp, but the beating, blow after blow, was being delivered in a ramshackle hut. Harriet even seemed to know the characters. The slave was a man like Josiah Henson, a Christian so true that he could grieve for his master's sins. And the master might have been the man with the iron fist whom Charles had met in Louisiana.

Harriet was so shaken by this experience that when she went home, she wrote it all out, including the dialogue, which she seemed to have heard as she sat on the church bench. She wrote at top speed, and when she ran out of paper, she reached for brown wrapping paper and continued on that. She called the slave Tom. The master was Simon Legree, originally from New England, which was important to the story. This was one way to make clear that slavery was not just a Southern evil; it was a national evil. It was amazing to her that it could go on and on. And with the permission of the American law! Within sight of the Church!

When she had finished writing, Harriet still didn't know what to do with her piece. It was the same length as her usual sketches, but it presented such a violent picture, she knew she couldn't fling it at her readers so abruptly, with neither preparation or explanation. It wouldn't do. She left the quickly scratched-out words on the desk for almost a month.

Then in early March, Calvin came home. In his usual orderly fashion he was putting his things away when he came upon the manuscript. Going from the first papers to the wrapping paper, he read it all. Obviously moved, he asked Harriet what this was about.

And she told him.

"You must go on with it," Calvin said. He sounded as sure of himself as Henry Ward ever did. "You must make up a story with this for the climax. The Lord intends it so."

Harriet saw in a flash that she could go on. She would tell it all in pictures, just as she had told about Tom's death. She wrote to the editor of the magazine she'd been dealing with, the *National Era*. She was working on a story about slavery, she said, which would show all sides of it. But she warned him: the story might go on for three or four issues.

Dr. Bailey, the editor, was interested. He offered her $300 for a serial in three or four installments.

So Harriet began.

CHAPTER SIX

Harriet lived in two worlds now—one with her family, one with the set of characters she was creating for her story. If Henry Ward had been there, he would have said that Harriet was "owling about," for she was distracted, reaching back into that "gathering" memory of hers where all the people and scenes were waiting. Although she had never lived in the South, in her Cincinnati years she had accumulated a wealth of stories or snippets of stories firsthand, some from her brother Charles, others from reading and listening to accounts by fugitive slaves. One of her best sources was her cook in Cincinnati, Eliza Buck, a former slave, married to a slave. All she had to do was to arrange all this material into story form and breathe life into it. Once started, however, she was driven by her emotions. All those pent-up feelings she had said had "burned inward" poured feverishly out, page after page. Pausing neither for breath nor punctuation, she littered her papers with dashes and then moved on. She *became* her characters, living through their troubles as if they were her own.

She couldn't stop. The first installment appeared on June 5, 1851, with the title *Uncle Tom's Cabin.* At first she used the

subtitle *The Man Who Was a Thing*. To Harriet the most
horrendous aspect of slavery was the fact that a slave really
was a "thing," a piece of property that could be sold like a
barrel of flour. Before the issue was printed, however, the
subtitle was changed to *Life Among the Lowly*. Now there
were deadlines to meet. Harriet wrote furiously at the kitchen
table until her father came to visit. He brought his work with
him—a bag full of old sermons he was editing for a book.
When he spread them over the kitchen table, Harriet picked
up her papers, moved to the back steps, and wrote on her lap.
Chapter followed chapter until Harriet wondered if in spite of
herself she was writing a novel. Her publisher wondered too.
In any case, her readers could hardly wait for the next installment and objected if she missed a deadline.

In August Catharine arrived. She was fifty-one years old
now and as full of schemes as ever. Why shouldn't she and
Harriet start a small boarding school in Harriet's home? she
suggested. Knowing Catharine, Calvin would certainly have
urged Harriet to say no, but she didn't. Perhaps she felt sorry
for Catharine, who was forever running into trouble with the
family. In any case, Harriet agreed, and that was all that
Catharine needed. She plunged ahead. She ordered a new
furnace ($150), planned for partitions to be put up in the
house, decided a new carpet was indispensable. To her sister
Mary, she wrote, "You know [Calvin] Stowe has a monoma-
nia about running into debt." She quieted him by taking all
the risk herself. She promised to pay any bills that were not
met by the income from the students.

A few months later Calvin must have said, "I told you so."
(Probably he said a great deal more.) Catharine was complaining that though she had offered to help with Harriet's

t would be". It aint the first time I've been out in
he night, carrying water to such as you"

"Thank you missis, says Tom when he has done
drinking"

"Dont call me, missis— I'm a miserable
slave like yourself— a lower one than you can ever
be", said she bitterly,— but now said she, going
to the door, & dragging in a small pallaise on
which she has spread linen cloths wet with water
try my poor fellow to roll yourself onto this.—

Stiff with wounds & bruises, Tom was a long
time in accomplishing this movement, but when done
he felt a sensible relief from the cooling application
to his wounds.

The woman, whom long practice with the
victims of brutality, had made familiar with many
healing arts, went on to make many applications
to Tom's wounds by means of which he was soon
somewhat relieved.

"Now said the woman, when she had raised
his head on a roll of damaged cotton which
serves for a pillow — there's the best I can do
for you.

Tom thanks her, & the woman sitting down
on the floor, drew up her knees & embracing them
with her arms, looked fixedly at him before
her, with a bitter & painful expression of countenance

Her bonnet fell back & long wavy stream....

Manuscript page from Uncle Tom's Cabin

project and had done much of the work, Harriet was taking all the profit.

Whose project? Harriet was indignant. The project, she said in a letter to Catharine, "arose from yourself. . . . I had at the time very serious doubts about your ability to carry it through." As for profit, she didn't see that there would be *any* profit. She just hoped that she wouldn't run into too much debt.

Catharine also took over *Uncle Tom* as if it were a joint project. Seeing that Harriet had so many interruptions at home, she "sent" her to work at Calvin's college office. Catharine wanted to get *Uncle Tom* "out of the way," she told her sister Mary. And when she saw that the installments were growing to book length, she approached her own publisher on the matter. He wasn't interested, but when Harriet and Calvin signed a contract with a Boston publisher, Catharine was infuriated. Harriet didn't know how to manage this sort of thing, she said. She had been cheated. Although Harriet was promised the standard ten percent royalty, Catharine insisted that it wasn't enough. It *was* enough, Harriet said. She was satisfied, but that didn't stop Catharine. Even when Harriet begged her not to interfere, Catharine went right on interfering. She threatened to create a public scandal about the publisher and, as the Beechers knew, she was capable of doing it. Mary told her father how she had entreated Catharine to be still, but "all we can say passes by like the wind." Only the combined pressure of the Beecher family made Catharine finally keep quiet.

The important thing, however, was that Harriet had finished *Uncle Tom.* She was forty-one years old and she had done what she had wanted to do. *Uncle Tom* was her personal declaration. And in a strange way the writing had set her free. All those emotions she had stamped down had found their way into words, and she was as free as any fugitive who crossed into Canada. Now she waited to see what *Uncle Tom's Cabin* would do. On the one hand, she prayed that the book would bring peace to the nation. If slave owners saw slavery for what it really was, she reasoned, how could they have anything more to do with it? On the other hand, she hoped that at least she'd make enough money to buy a silk dress.

What she didn't know was that she had stepped right into American literature. Without realizing it, Harriet Beecher Stowe had written America's first protest novel, the first book written against a law. She meant it to be realistic. "In a novel," she commented, "people's hearts broke, and they die, and that is the end of it; and in a story this is very convenient. But in real life we do not die." It was real life that she was writing about, and if she did not achieve the sophistication of a truly realistic novel, she did make her scenes come alive with local color and specific detail. Still, Harriet could be sentimental in the style of her time; she could be "preachy"; but she could also strike off a commanding sentence and deliver a sarcastic dig. "If any of our refined and Christian readers," she wrote, "object to the society into which this scene introduces them, let us beg them to . . . conquer their prejudices. The catching [slaves] business . . . is rising to the dignity of a lawful and patriotic profession." Most important, Harriet had done what she wanted to do: she had used a novel to criticize and denounce a society.

Uncle Tom's Cabin was published on March 20, 1852. The publisher must have known that Harriet's characters were believable, her plot fast-paced, and her subject timely, yet

"Eliza Crossing the Ice" from Uncle Tom's Cabin

never in his wildest dreams did he foresee that *Uncle Tom's Cabin* would be an immediate smash hit. By mid-June 10,000 copies of the book were being sold every week. In order to keep up with the demand, the publisher had three power presses running twenty-four hours a day, one hundred and twenty-five to two hundred bookbinders at work, and three mills going full tilt to supply the paper. Six months after publication, 150,000 copies had been sold. The book was published and sold equally well overseas, although neither Harriet nor her publisher profited from this. In order to receive royalties, a writer had to be on English soil when applying for an English copyright, and of course Harriet wasn't there.

But she was certainly well known. In America senators, poets, and scholars, as well as everyday folks, were praising her. Henry Wadsworth Longfellow, the poet, wrote to her, congratulating her on "one of the greatest triumphs recorded in literary history, to say nothing of the higher triumph of its moral effect." High praise as this was, Harriet would have been even more impressed had she read his diary. "At one step," he wrote, "she has reached the top of the staircase up which the rest of us climb on our knees year after year."

And for the first time in her life Harriet had money— $10,300 at the end of three months. She had no reason to pinch pennies now and she wasn't going to. She hired a cook, a governess, and a housekeeper, and in preparation for a trip to Boston, Hartford, and New York, she bought herself (surely!) at least one silk dress. She would need such dresses, for wherever she went on her trip she would find herself in the midst of a social whirl. Everyone wanted to meet the famous Mrs. Stowe and, it seemed to Harriet, everyone did. What she most enjoyed, however, was visiting with her family. Her father, living in Boston now, made what he thought was a joke. They all better watch out, he said, laughing. Harriet might become more famous than he was! Harriet must have smiled.

Serious-minded Edward was more wary about her fame. He was afraid that all this attention would turn her head and make her vain. Harriet knew there was no danger. Hard as she had worked, she didn't feel that she could take much credit for *Uncle Tom's Cabin.* It seemed to her that the book had always been there. All she had done was find it and take down the words.

In New York Harriet was entertained and fussed over by members of Henry Ward's church. She was taken to a concert where the famous Jenny Lind was singing. She helped Henry Ward raise money to buy the freedom of two slaves, daughters of a free black woman whom he knew. On Sundays Harriet went to church and heard this favorite brother of hers in all his glory, weaving a spell that bound his congregation together in love for him. Surely Henry Ward must have been proud of Harriet's success; surely he said so. But he hadn't read her book. Nor would he for at least a year.

In the midst of Harriet's crowded interlude in New York, she wrote to Calvin. "It is not fame nor praise that contents me," she wrote. "I seem never to have needed love so much. I long to hear you say how much you love me."

In June Harriet returned to Brunswick, taking with her Isabella Hooker, her thirty-year-old half sister, who promised to help Harriet with her large volume of mail. Although Isabella had once complained of her "insipid" everyday life, she felt uneasy in Harriet's company. In comparison with Harriet's genius, she wrote her husband, her own littleness fairly stared her in the face! Isabella, a natural leader, was at the point in her life where Harriet had once been. All the Beechers (except Mary) were compelled to make a declaration of some sort, and Isabella had not found yet what hers was to be. Meanwhile she told her husband to take comfort in the fact that she would not be half as good a *wife* if she had Harriet's gifts. "One cannot do forty things at once," she said.

But Harriet had always tried to do those forty things. Now she was getting ready to move again. The move to Andover was scheduled for the fall, when Calvin would begin teaching, but Harriet was going on ahead to arrange their living quarters. All her adult life Harriet had lived in rented houses, where she had to make do with arrangements as she found them. Always she had longed to have a place where she could begin from scratch and have everything just as she liked it. So when she was shown the house intended for the Stowes, she resisted. What about that stone building she'd seen on the campus? she asked. It looked empty. Once used as a carpenter shop and then as a gymnasium, the stone building was indeed empty, but the trustees didn't think they could afford to remodel it. When Harriet offered to pay for it herself, the trustees consented. When the house was done, they'd pay her back.

It was a happy summer for Harriet. She loved planning the house, supervising the workmen, meeting the faculty at Andover. The place had everything that Brunswick had, she wrote Calvin. Except the sea; she loved the sea. But the elm trees almost made up for that. Harriet sketched them and promised that one day they would make their way into a book of hers. The family joined Harriet in September, but "The Stone Cabin," as Harriet called it, was not ready until December.

Although Harriet continued to be deluged with mail, the tone of some of the letters was changing. Southerners who had at first thought of *Uncle Tom's Cabin* as simply a story

Stowe House, Andover, MA

began to see the book for what it was. What did Mrs. Stowe know about the South? they asked. She was just another obnoxious abolitionist, they said, flooding the South with more of the North's hate propaganda. Southern critics talked of Mrs. Stowe's "foul imagination" and referred to her book as "revolting," "slanderous," "loathsome." One anonymous Southern writer enclosed a human ear in his letters. A black ear. Indeed, Mrs. Stowe was so despised that children in Richmond, Virginia, sang a kind of jump-rope song about her in the streets.

"Go, go, go,
Ol' Harriet Beecher Stowe!
We don't want you here in Virginny—
Go, go, go!"

What aggravated Harriet most was that these people didn't *believe* she knew what she was talking about! They thought she'd made it all up. They wouldn't listen. "What man has nerve to do," she once said, "man had not nerve to hear." She'd have to *prove* the truth. She'd write *A Key to Uncle Tom's Cabin,* listing all the specific sources, showing just where each incident had come from, citing examples to back up what she'd written. It took Harriet three months to finish her *Key.* It sold, as everything Mrs. Stowe would write these days would sell, but it didn't change Southern minds.

Uncle Tom's Cabin was not bringing peace to the nation. Instead it added fuel to the fire that was building. But Harriet knew now what she had to do. She'd have to keep working until the job was done. There was nothing "intermediate" about her now. Her cause was one with that of the famous senator Charles Sumner, who so often quoted *Uncle Tom's Cabin* in his speeches. She was almost to the point of going along with William Lloyd Garrison, that ultra of ultras among the abolitionists.

And she was going to have the chance to spread the word. In the spring of 1853 she and Calvin were invited (all expenses paid) to talk with antislavery societies in the British Isles. "The public opinion of the world is our last hope," she wrote Senator Sumner, and she hoped to strengthen that opinion.

But that was not the only reason she was excited. Just think of the sights she'd see! She could visit Shakespeare's grave! She could walk the streets that Sir Walter Scott had walked! And after England and Scotland, why couldn't they extend their trip to Paris? To the Alps? Why not?

CHAPTER SEVEN

Harriet and Calvin invited Charles Beecher to go with them to Europe. As interested in art and music as he was, he would, of all the Beechers, enjoy the trip most, they thought. In addition, he could act as Harriet's secretary, answering letters, keeping a diary, arranging travel plans. And since Calvin had to be back at Andover by May or June, Charles could take over the public speeches that, as a lady, Harriet could not give in mixed company. Three more Beechers asked to go along—Sarah, George's widow, who had money enough to pay her own expenses and those of her son, George, and her brother, William. The Stowes placed their children in various schools and with relatives, and on March 30, 1853, the party of six set sail from Boston for Liverpool, England.

At first Harriet was seasick, complaining of the eternal cradlelike rocking of the ship. But determined to enjoy the trip, she soon joined the others at their favorite spot, huddled around the ship's red smokestack. Wrapped against the cold in all the clothes they could find, they sang. Right into the teeth of the Atlantic wind, they sang. One of their favorites was "Amazing Grace." Its simple melody rode fearless over the water.

They first sighted land at Kinsale Point on the south shore

of Ireland. For Charles and Harriet this was a place they had never seen but would never forget. It was here that Catharine's fiancé had drowned so many years ago. They could see the very rock his ship had struck before going down. And to this day they carried the vivid memory of Catharine thrown across her bed, sobbing her heart out. It took her two years to recover, and for the rest of the Beecher children there seemed no greater tragedy than to drown or to love someone who had drowned. Charles couldn't help but remark in his diary how different Catharine might have been, had it not been for that rock. Now Catharine was a pathetic sight, "a mind too strong for her frail body and driving it as an engine drives a shattered boat."

At nine o'clock in the morning of April 10, they arrived in Liverpool. The American flag was hoisted on their ship. Guns from the shore welcomed the incoming vessel. This was *England,* Harriet told herself. As their ship threaded its way through the forest of masts along the waterfront, the crowd on the dock looked like any Boston crowd, except it was larger.

As it turned out, however, this crowd wasn't at all like a Boston crowd. When their Liverpool hosts met them and guided them through the crowd, the people backed up, made a path for them, then turned to watch every step they took. This crowd had come to see *Harriet Beecher Stowe.* They craned their necks and whispered, "There she is. The one with the curls." Even when Harriet's party was ushered into two separate carriages, the people lined up beside Harriet's carriage, staring. Harriet glanced through her window at Charles in the second carriage. She caught his eye and laughed. "Isn't this funny?" she seemed to say. "Can you believe it?"

Harriet had been warned that there would be large meetings

and parties in her honor, but she had not been prepared for the crowds that turned out on the streets just to watch her pass. If someone in a village called out, "Mrs. Stowe," every door would fly open and out they would pour—the butcher, the baker covered with flour, the housewife with one child in her arms, others hanging on to her skirt. In store windows there were pictures of Harriet, or rather pictures of someone who was supposed to look like Harriet.

"I declare," Harriet laughed, "if the people *want* to look at me, I don't see why they shouldn't." Plain as she believed herself to be, she knew she was an improvement over the pictures, which might as well have been of the Egyptian Sphinx.

The Harriet of the early Cincinnati days, who shrank from public attention, would have been amazed at this Harriet, who accepted the cheers of Scottish and English audiences as if she'd been born famous but was secretly amused at the commotion she was causing. The audiences were always large—2,000 to 4,000—and at the very sight of Harriet they went wild, cheering, stamping, hurrahing, waving hats and umbrellas and anything else that came to hand. The private parties were almost as large and more daunting, for then Harriet had to mix with the people and make friends with strangers—dukes and duchesses among them, lords and ladies. But whatever the circumstances, Charles said Harriet was "brave as a lion." Harriet put it differently. She said she was "tame as a lion." She just did whatever was expected of her.

At the end of each day, when the six travelers met privately, they reviewed all that had happened. "Did you call a duchess 'Your Grace' or 'Your ladyship?' " they asked. Harriet said she didn't call them anything. That was safest. They teased

Calvin, who was forever making mistakes in this high company. Once he walked off from a party with someone else's overcoat; once he forgot his hat. And once he all but spilled a bowl of soup in the lap of a duchess. Charles concluded, however, that they had behaved pretty well. They ate with gold spoons off silver plates, and when they were served strawberries as big as eggs, they never let on that New England strawberries might be smaller.

All the same, Harriet did make friends, particularly with the Duchess of Sutherland, a warm, informal woman who was obviously drawn to Harriet and eager to support the anti-slavery movement. She gave Harriet a gold ten-linked slave bracelet with two of the links inscribed with the dates when the English had freed their slaves in the West Indies. The other links were to be inscribed with the dates when America's slaves were freed. Soon, they all hoped.

As busy as their schedule was, however, they did see the sights. When they came to the statue of Sir Walter Scott standing in the center of Edinburgh, Charles and Harriet felt they had run into an old friend. He was the only novelist of whom Lyman Beecher approved, so the children knew his books almost as well as the Bible. Charles said he didn't see why the old gentleman didn't step down from his pedestal and shake their hands. Later, when they visited his mansion, Harriet insisted that they see it by moonlight. That was the way that Scott himself had pictured it, but since the moon didn't rise until after midnight, the others preferred to skip the romance. Still, Harriet insisted.

Nothing discouraged her. Not even the rain and mud when they reached Stratford-upon-Avon, Shakespeare's old stamping ground. Calvin had been here before; Charles was frankly

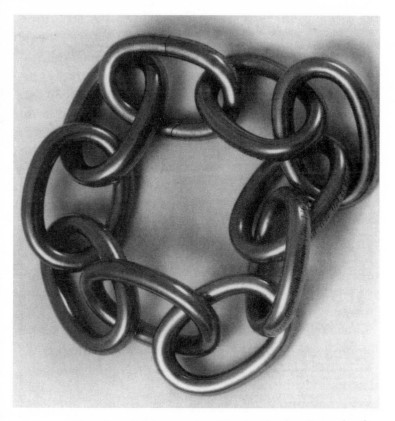

Slave bracelet presented to Harriet Beecher Stowe by the Duchess of Sutherland, May 7, 1853

bored; but in spite of the crowds that followed her, Harriet felt only the presence of Shakespeare. As she walked through the church gardens that Shakespeare once knew, she picked an ivy leaf, a sprig of holly, a bit of moss to press in the memory book she was making. Even the weather probably did not keep her from counting this a "white day." It was how they described an especially memorable day.

The people who thronged to meetings and parties for Harriet did not come only out of curiosity. They seemed truly to want to help. Wherever she went, Harriet was given money to use, as she put it, for the *cause*. In England alone she collected $50,000; in Scotland she was given $750 in one place and a cup filled with gold pieces in another. The most impressive gift, however, was a set of twenty-six white leather-bound books filled with the signatures of half a million British women who appealed to the women of America to speak out against the evil of slavery. As well intentioned as the appeal was, the wording annoyed Calvin. Americans didn't need to be told that slavery was evil. They didn't need to to be reminded that slavery was against the teachings of Christ. Yes, of course, Great Britain had freed their slaves in the West Indies, but that was easy. They only had a few thousand slaves and freeing them had little effect on their economy.

Calvin found it difficult to contain himself at public meetings when speakers did nothing but denounce America for its wickedness. Finally, at a particularly crowded meeting in London, Calvin could hold back no longer. Speaker after speaker had ripped into America. The audience had hissed and hooted and howled to show their contempt for America's sins. Then one speaker had quoted the new American president, Franklin Pierce, who had promised to enforce the Fugitive Slave Law. As in one voice, everyone in the hall had shouted, "Shame! Shame!"

Calvin was as disappointed as anyone in Pierce's stand. After all, Franklin Pierce had been Calvin's classmate at Bowdoin College, but it was one thing for Americans to attack him and another thing for the English to do it. Besides, the British, no matter how superior they acted, were partially responsible for slavery in America. The cotton-growing

The Scott Monument, Edinburgh, Scotland

plantations in America were the ones that used and abused slavery the most. And who bought that cotton? The English. They bought four-fifths of American cotton. If the English really wanted to stop American slavery, Calvin pointed out, all they had to do was to quit buying. It was a brave but, of course, an unpopular speech.

Ten days later Calvin was on his way to Liverpool and from there to Andover. Sarah, George, and William had long since tired of trailing after a celebrity and were in Italy, planning to rejoin the others in Switzerland. Harriet sympathized with Sarah's impatience with crowds. How often had she longed to be alone where she did not have to *"see* anything or *say* anything!" Charles summed up all their feelings. As exciting as their trip had been, it had not been *"play."*

But now they were ready for play. Harriet and Charles arrived in France on June 4, and before the day was over Charles had decided that French life was different from English life. In England you did what other people wanted you to do; in France you did as you pleased. Charles, who had had a taste of French life in New Orleans, fell in love with Paris and left reluctantly for Switzerland, where the other three would be waiting. He didn't relish the idea of trudging up and down mountains for a month, but someone, he figured, would have to make sure that Harriet didn't break her neck.

And there were times when it seemed quite possible that a neck might be broken. Once their carriage tipped over on a mountain road and they all had to be pulled out from under,

Calvin Ellis Stowe

but except for a few bruises, no harm was done. Most of the time they ascended mountains single file on the back of mules who were forever stretching over the edge of a precipice for a tasty morsel to eat. The ladies might squeal, but whatever happened, they'd soon be laughing. It was as if they were really saying, "Isn't this *fun?* Just look where we are!"

Harriet, who had once been overwhelmed by Niagara Falls, was in raptures at the sight of snowcapped mountain peaks competing to catch the first rays of the morning sun. Charles, who had at first been so indifferent to the mountains, became almost poetic in his descriptions, but when Harriet and William wanted Charles to see yet another glacier, he refused. He'd rather stay at the hotel, he said. "Stupid! Stupid fellow!" Harriet cried over her shoulder as she rode off. Charles believed in taking the Alps in moderation, but Harriet! She skipped up and down the high places and when she reached a glacier, she sat right down at the edge and went into a trance.

Harriet was indeed transported by all she saw in Europe, not only the scenery and the historic spots, but the art as well. In New England, she wrote, one was not allowed to enjoy beauty for its own sake, so "the soul withered and was crushed. I know because I have felt it." She was forty-three years old when she returned to Andover in September 1853. Her twin daughters were seventeen, Henry would soon be entering Dartmouth College, Fred was thirteen, Georgiana (or Georgie) was ten years old, and little Charley was four. And Harriet was going to make sure that they were not raised in a crushing atmosphere. The Stone Cabin became the center of social life, evenings of music, parties, charades, and literary gatherings.

But of course Harriet's primary concern was slavery. She

was considered a leader in the antislavery movement, and for her it had become a do-or-die matter. She would do until slavery died or until she did. She signed her letters now "Yours for the cause." She thought of Senator Sumner as a personal friend, and now William Lloyd Garrison, that "ultra of ultras," turned to Harriet. Once many years ago he had asked Lyman Beecher for support, but Lyman had refused in an offhand manner that Garrison had resented. Lyman had "too many irons in the fire," he had said. But Garrison figured that Lyman's daughter and he both had their irons in the same fire, and apparently Harriet agreed. At least she invited him to the Stone Cabin for two days in December and decided that aside from his negative attitude toward the church, he wasn't too ultra for her, after all. He might be "the celebrated wolf of all wolves," she said, but she thought he was just "a sheep in wolf's cloth."

But in January 1854 the nation was suddenly flung into such an emergency that whatever their differences, the antislavery forces drew together. The territory of Kansas and Nebraska wanted to be admitted to the Union. The North took for granted that Kansas would be a free state. After all, as long ago as 1820, Congress had agreed on the Missouri Compromise, which had drawn a line through the territories, ruling that no new state north of this line could be admitted as a slave state. Kansas and Nebraska were north of this line, but suddenly the South refused to abide by the Missouri Compromise. Instead, Southern congressmen proposed that the new states decide for themselves whether they wanted to be slave or free.

Although this scheme might sound democratic, Northerners saw it for the tricky business it was. Kansas was right next door to Missouri, and the western border of Missouri was settled by a rough crowd prepared to fight for slavery. By the time the slavery question came to a vote, enough Missourians would have crossed over to Kansas, and by hook or crook they would make sure that the United States had one more slave state. That would be the beginning of the end, Northerners said—the first step to legalizing slavery throughout the country.

The only hope was to defeat the Kansas-Nebraska Bill before it became an Act. Harriet swung into action. She would get up a petition against the bill signed by every preacher in New England. Congress ought to listen when the Church (Catholics included) spoke in one voice. She wrote Senator Sumner, asking him to hold off any vote until the petition arrived. While Harriet wrote letters, Edward, Calvin, and even old Lyman himself joined other petitioners, scouring the New England countryside for signatures. In the end, 3,050 preachers signed the petition, which when delivered to Congress was two hundred feet long. For once, Harriet said, the Church had not disappointed her.

Then she turned to the women of America. She addressed them in a bold headline in a prominent magazine, *The Independent*. "Women of the Free States!" she cried. "Shall every State be thrown open as a slave State?" Women could no longer be genteel, she told them. They could no longer be silent about politics as they had been taught to do. They should think of their children. And their children's children! Did they want a slave depot in New York? Speak out!

But neither the clergy nor women nor Senator Sumner nor the shrill voice of William Lloyd Garrison changed the minds of Southern congressmen. In May the Kansas-Nebraska Bill was voted into law. Now the question passed to Kansas itself. Would it vote free or slave? Just as everyone expected, those

Lyman Beecher

Missourians had moved in, ready to settle the issue by force, and indeed a mini-civil war had developed in the state. Henry Ward Beecher sent the freedom fighters barrels of rifles, which he called "Beecher Bibles," but there was one Eastern abolitionist who was truly a "do-or-die" man. John Brown brought his sons with him and he was prepared to kill.

Harriet decided that the best she could do was to start

another novel on slavery. Senator Sumner encouraged her. "We need your help at once in our struggle," he wrote. In May 1856, while she was writing, Senator Sumner delivered a fiery speech in which he attacked Senator Butler, a South Carolina senator and pro-slavery leader. As it happened, Senator Butler had a hotheaded young relative in Congress who believed that Senator Sumner had dishonored his family's name. He might have challenged Senator Sumner to a duel but he didn't bother. He walked down the aisle of the Senate to where Senator Sumner was sitting. He raised his gold-topped cane and brought it down on the senator's head. Not just once but time and again. He went on beating until his cane (all but the gold top) was shattered and until Senator Sumner lay unconscious on the floor in a pool of blood. For days Senator Sumner hovered between life and death, and although he did live, he never completely recovered. As for the young man with the cane, he became an instant hero in the South.

Three days later John Brown and his sons murdered five pro-slavery men in Kansas.

The fires were mounting. Harriet was halfway through her novel, which she was calling *Dred,* but after the attack on her friend Senator Sumner, the tone of her writing changed. There was no way that she could keep her hate out of the story. Nor did she try.

CHAPTER EIGHT

Although Dred, the hero of Harriet's new book, was an improbable character who walked out of the swamps, talking in Biblical language, her heroine was based on someone who in real life was as improbable as anyone Harriet could have dreamed up. Sojourner Truth, a Negro prophetess who toured the North giving speeches, had once out of curiosity called on Harriet. She had walked in, unannounced, on a family party in celebration of Lyman's eightieth birthday, and she had stolen the show. A tall, regal-looking woman, she spoke in a deep unearthly voice as if she were delivering the word of God in His own words. Harriet was so fascinated that she put a disguised Sojourner in her book.

With this book Harriet was going to make sure that she was in England in time to secure the copyright to the English publication. Harriet had promised her Boston publisher that she would finish the book before she left for England on July 30, 1856, but hard as she worked, she couldn't manage more than twenty handwritten pages a day. On July 30 there was still more to be written, but fortunately the voyage was smooth and she kept on writing. By the time she reached London, she had finished.

"It's done! and I send it," she wrote her publisher. "Congratulate me! I hardly thought I'd do it, but it's done and it *suits* me."

Accompanying Harriet on this European trip were Calvin, seventeen-year-old Henry (her favorite child), her sister Mary, and the twins who were to attend a finishing school in Paris. Harriet planned to stay in Europe for a year, but soon after her copyright had been attended to, Calvin returned to Andover. And in October young Henry left to enter the freshman class at Dartmouth—a month late because Harriet couldn't bear to part with him sooner.

Meanwhile *Dred* had been published both in the United States and in England, and although the critics were not as enthusiastic as they had been about *Uncle Tom's Cabin,* the book sold well. The shrill tone she had, perhaps unconsciously, used in the second half of the book did not sit well with reviewers. If in her first book she had occasionally been sarcastic about the response of the Church to slavery, now she was downright bitter. Some English critics accused her of being antireligious. Harriet—antireligious! How could she take such criticism seriously? In any case, 100,000 copies sold in four weeks. "After that," she wrote Calvin, "who cares what critics say?"

The year went by quickly, with Harriet visiting old friends and making new ones. On her return in July 1857, she was relieved that no catastrophe had occurred in America or in her family. Georgie, Freddie, and young Charley were fine, happy to be reunited with their mother. But if all seemed well in the world at the moment, it did not stay that way. A few weeks later there was terrible news. Not a national tragedy, a personal one. A telegram arrived from Dartmouth College.

Henry Ellis Stowe

Henry had drowned in the Connecticut River.

No! Not Henry! Not drowned!

Harriet had thought she knew what heartbreak was, but this was the worst thing that had happened to her. The worst she could imagine. It was as if she herself had been sucked under water, where she was forced to watch young Henry struggling, struggling, and then giving up. She too felt like giving up. She went through the motions of living, but all the time she was groping for solid ground.

Henry's classmates brought his body to Andover and explained how it had happened. He and two friends had swum across the Connecticut River from the New Hampshire side to the Vermont side. At this point the river was treacherous to cross in a single, nonstop effort. It was necessary to head for a sandbar in the middle of the river, rest, and then go on. They had no trouble on the way over, but going back, Henry apparently couldn't find the sandbar and was swept by the current down the river—down and under. His friends had tried to rescue him, but it happened too suddenly and was over so soon.

The explanation only made the terrible scene more vivid, more unbearable. Slowly Harriet did find a measure of peace, but never of forgetfulness. From time to time she would be attacked by waves of memory that all but paralyzed her. More than a year later, overcome by such a spell, she wrote, "I let my plants die by inches before my eyes and do not water them. I dread everything I do, and wish it was not to be done."

By this time Harriet had discovered that the best way for her to deal with emotion was not to suppress it but to express it. So she started another novel. The hero in this one *(The Minister's Wooing)* was a sailor who was drowned at sea. The story was set in old-time New England, which Harriet knew better than anyone. The heroine was brought up in the Puritan way to obey and submit, and certainly Harriet knew about that. But at the moment no one knew better than Harriet how the mother of the drowned sailor felt. The book was hailed as another gripping novel, and if it had an improbably happy ending, no one seemed to object. Apparently Harriet could not bear to do away with her hero forever, so at the end she brought him back, explaining that his death at sea had been a false rumor. Who could blame her for that? Her friends on the new *Atlantic* magazine, which was running the book serially, were well pleased. James Russell Lowell, the editor, wrote: "You are one of the few persons lucky enough to be born with eyes in your head,—that is, with something behind the eyes which makes them of value."

And now Harriet was off to England again to secure the English copyright. She planned another long stay, for she enjoyed nothing more than visits with her literary friends, people she had read and admired long before meeting them. They were not just acquaintances but real friends who corresponded with her in her absence: George Eliot, John Ruskin, Lady Byron, Elizabeth Barrett Browning. In October she was in Italy, seeing the Brownings, when she heard about the latest rampage of John Brown, that fanatical abolitionist who had led the massacre in Kansas.

John Brown had decided to free the slaves himself. Impatient with how slowly freedom was proceeding, he had brought his sons and a few friends to Harpers Ferry, Virginia, determined to take the United States arsenal there. Once he had the guns, he planned to give them out to slaves to fight for their freedom. He figured that an army of four million slaves would gather quickly. It was a harebrained idea with no possi-

Robert Browning

Elizabeth Barrett Browning

bility of success, and John Brown's sons told him so. Where would the slaves come from? How would they know? How could a handful of men defeat the United States Army? Brown brushed the arguments aside. He was doing the work of God, he said, and God would take care of the details. At first it looked as if God really were helping to carry out this impossible mission. On Sunday morning, October 16, 1859, John Brown managed not only to surprise those on guard at the arsenal but to capture it as well. Moreover, he held it until Tuesday, when Major Robert E. Lee and United States forces descended on Harpers Ferry and brought the siege to an end. And what had happened in those two days? John Brown had been wounded and two sons killed. And that was all.

Had John Brown himself been killed, he might have been

John Brown

dismissed as that crazy man who had gone on a killing spree in Kansas. But there was no way to forget John Brown, who lay wounded in jail, talking reasonably, granting interviews to newspapers, behaving with dignity, quoting from the Bible. He was eloquent at his trial, and when he was hanged, he died magnificently—bravely, proudly, and without repenting. To the North he became a hero who towered above other heroes, a man to write songs about. Emerson called him a "saint." Harriet called him a "great quiet spirit."

But to Southerners John Brown was a fiend, a terrorist, the first of many who undoubtedly planned to swoop down on them from the North. Slaveholders put a price on the head of every abolitionist who had praised John Brown. Frederick Douglass, the famous Negro educator, fearing for his life, fled to England. And Henry Ward Beecher stayed close to home. If he put one foot into slave territory, he was told, he'd find himself hanging from the nearest tree. Members of Congress from both the North and the South were in such a state of hysteria that they armed themselves before attending sessions.

When Harriet arrived home from England at the end of June 1860, she probably had no idea how close the country teetered on the edge of war. Southerners openly declared that the only way the North could keep the South from seceding from the Union was to abandon the antislavery movement. The South simply would not and could not take any more abuse. The question of secession hung on the next presidential election. If a Northern Republican won, the South put the country on notice: it would quit. If the North wanted a war, let them have it.

The nominee for the Northern Republicans was Abraham Lincoln, and on November 6, 1860, his election was announced. He would not take office until March 4, but the South did not wait. South Carolina led the way, seceding on December 20. In the next month six more states seceded and formed their own government under the leadership of Jefferson Davis.

To Abraham Lincoln nothing was as important as holding the Union together, but if there was going to be a war, he announced, he was not going to be the one to start it.

He didn't need to. On Friday, April 12, 1861, a Southern general, Pierre Beauregard, fired on Fort Sumter, a federal fort in Charleston, South Carolina. The fort fell to the South and on Sunday, April 14, the American flag was lowered. War had begun.

Harriet was not unduly upset. Better a war, she said, than slavery. And like nearly everyone in both the North and South, she figured the war would be a short one.

CHAPTER NINE

Many of the Beechers helped to bring about the Civil War and many fought in it. One of the first to enlist was Henry Ward's oldest son, twenty-year-old Henry. When he asked his father's permission to join, Henry Ward said he'd better join if he didn't want to be disowned. Another of Henry Ward's sons also went and Charles Beecher's son, Fred. But when Harriet's son, Fred, wanted to join, Harriet was hesitant. She worried about him. She wouldn't admit it, but she suspected that he had a problem with alcohol. She had recently sent him to a water cure in Elmira, New York, near her brother Thomas, who had a church there. But Fred didn't stay long. Apparently he fell in with a bad crowd and Thomas sent him home. In any case, with or without permission, Fred did enlist and Harriet could only be proud.

James, who had been doing missionary work with sailors in Hong Kong, returned and enlisted in the 141st New York Volunteers, which Thomas had helped recruit. He advanced quickly to the rank of lieutenant colonel, but threatened with a nervous breakdown, he had to leave temporarily. On his return he recruited the First North Carolina Volunteers, the first all-black regiment from the South. This was perhaps his proudest accomplishment. He equipped the regiment, trained it, and led it, and if there were those who doubted that an all-black Southern regiment could perform well, all they had to do was watch his soldiers in action.

In 1862 Thomas joined James's New York Regiment as a chaplain, but he stayed only four months. Harriet called him "Thomas the Doubter" because he refused to do what was expected of him. As a minister, he wouldn't even dress like a minister in a black coat and white tie. Nor did he behave like

James Beecher

a minister. Around town he wore a cap with a visor, stopped off for a game of billiards, drank a glass of beer if he felt like it, and played baseball when he had the chance. He warned his congregation that he wouldn't make conventional pastoral calls but would be available to anyone who needed help, no matter what kind of help was needed—sawing wood, caring for the sick, moving furniture. His congregation, who adored him, allowed him to be himself. The army was a different matter. It didn't tolerate much individuality, and he couldn't tolerate the army. He went back to Elmira, where he continued to support the North in his own way.

The other Beechers joined the war on the sidelines. Isabella, just home from a water cure, still complained about how inept she was. Still, she was sure she had hidden talents. She felt she had it in her to "sweep people along on the right path," and talented or not, she swept every chance she had. The war was barely six months old when she wrote to Lincoln, pointing out the right path for him to take.

But the two most vocal spectators of the war were Harriet and Henry Ward. They both approved of President Lincoln's prompt order to blockade Southern ports. Of course this imposed a hardship on England. Deprived of Southern cotton, England would have to close down its cotton mills. But England wouldn't mind the sacrifice, Harriet supposed. After all, the English would do anything to wipe out slavery in the world. Certainly they had shown her their absolute support of the "cause," so she could hardly believe reports that England was leaning toward the South. Yet English ministers were asking why the North didn't just let the South go. Didn't the South have as much right to independence as America itself had once claimed that it had? Even Lord Shaftesbury, who had composed that famous antislavery petition for the half million women who signed, seemed to be treating the war as if it were just a political disagreement within the United States.

Harriet felt as if she had been stabbed in the back by her best friends. Why had the English given her such an overwhelming reception if they hadn't meant it? How could she trust England again? The English were even building ships, which they intended to use to break the blockade of the South. Did they mean to enter the war on the side of the South? If they did, Harriet knew, as everyone did, that this would be a fatal blow to the North.

The North was having trouble enough as it was. Battle after battle had been lost, until people were losing faith in both Lincoln and his generals. Even Lincoln was losing faith in his generals, particularly General George McClellan, who was constantly stalling, complaining that he was outnumbered, doing nothing. Thomas Beecher, who was serving as chaplain at this time, reportedly heard rumors that McClellan wanted to move into the White House and replace Lincoln. Thomas had known Lincoln in Illinois, and before he went back to Elmira, he is supposed to have called on Lincoln and told him the rumors. In any case, Lincoln did remove McClellan from his command. The next general, however, did no better. Nor the one after that.

Harriet and Henry Ward knew why the North was doing so poorly. Lincoln hadn't freed the slaves. He hadn't even talked about freeing them. He hadn't made the war sound like the righteous war that it was. In August 1861, when General John Frémont fought in Missouri and personally freed the slaves in all the territory that he captured, what did Lincoln do? He

Harriet Beecher Stowe, Lyman Beecher,
and Henry Ward Beecher

said Frémont had no authority to free slaves and he removed
Frémont from his post. Harriet and Henry Ward were out-
raged and didn't hesitate to say so. Henry Ward even gave a
big dinner to honor General Frémont.

All Lincoln talked about was preserving the Union, and
whether the abolitionists realized it or not, he had reasons for

not talking about slaves. If he expected to win this war, he had to be careful about those slave-owning border states that still sided with the North. Any talk about freeing slaves, and those border states would certainly switch sides. Lincoln was walking a tightrope, and Harriet and Henry Ward did not make it easier.

The two of them attacked the president in language so scorching they sounded like Lyman Beecher.

"Union, union, union!" Harriet cried. That's all she heard. What about emancipation? What about the "voice of the Lord"?

Henry Ward accused Lincoln of being more interested in politics than in the success of the war. "We have a Country," he cried. "We have a Cause. We have a People. Let all good men pray that God gives us a Government!"

Thomas warned Henry that so much talk of emancipation was doing the country no good. Average Northern soldiers, he said, were not fighting to free slaves. They were fighting to beat the South and to keep the country together. But slaves? Abolitionists might care but not the common soldier. Thomas had recruited soldiers and knew what he was talking about.

Yet of course Lincoln did care about the slaves. He planned to talk about emancipation but only in the right way and at the right time. He wanted to wait until the North had scored a victory. If people thought the North was winning, there was a better chance of the states' sticking together. That victory, however, was slow in coming. Still, in April 1862 Lincoln took a first step. He abolished slavery in the District of Columbia, offering to pay slaveholders for the loss of their slaves. In June 1862 he abolished slavery in all the territories. Then in September 1862, in Antietam, a little town in Maryland, the victory that Lincoln had been waiting for came about. Encouraged, Lincoln announced that if the South had not asked for peace by January 1, he would on that day sign an Emancipation Proclamation, freeing all slaves in those areas still in rebellion.

Of course this might not make much difference to the slaves in those areas. They would be under the control of their masters, no matter what Mr. Lincoln said. But to Harriet this Proclamation would make all the difference. It would announce to the world what the war was all about. It would let everyone know what kind of country America would be when the North had won. And now that emancipation was out in the open, she wanted to answer those half million British women who were so worried about the evil in America. She would make a public appeal to the women of Great Britain just as they had appealed to the American women.

Still, Harriet didn't quite trust Abraham Lincoln. Suppose he didn't keep his promise? Suppose he didn't sign the Proclamation after all? She decided to go to the White House and ask him point-blank. She arranged for an interview, and in November she took her daughter, twenty-six-year-old Hattie, and her twelve-year-old son, Charley, and went to Washington. Isabella, who apparently wanted to make sure that everyone took the right path, went along.

Harriet had known that the president was a tall, ungainly man with country ways, and when he unfolded his great length from his chair to greet them, she could see that he was all these. But she had not been prepared for his eyes. They seemed to hold all the sadness of the world in them. When he listened, he seemed to understand. When he spoke, he spoke from the heart.

According to the Beechers, the president smiled down at Harriet. "So this is the little lady who made this big war?" he said.

Lincoln assured Harriet that he would indeed sign the Proclamation, and he undoubtedly helped her understand the difficulties he was up against. In any case, Harriet was won over. Afterward Charley wanted to know why the president had said he'd always had a fire *"to* home" instead of *"at* home." When Hattie wrote her sister, she made fun of the interview, but Harriet's heart went out to the man. She believed all that he said, and whatever he did in the future, she would trust him.

She wrote a ten-page letter to British women and sent it to the *Atlantic* for publication. She ended it on the same note that the British women had used. She asked them to raise their voices "for the removal of this disgrace to the Christian world."

On January 1 Harriet went to the Boston Music Hall to attend a jubilee to celebrate the signing of the Emancipation Proclamation—or rather the expectation of its being signed. She took a back seat in the balcony and listened to Ralph Waldo Emerson read a poem and to several musical numbers, but at intermission there was still no official word from Washington. Then a gentleman in a full-dress suit stepped to the center of the stage.

"Ladies and gentlemen," he cried, "the telegraph has just brought the news from Washington." The president had signed the Emancipation Proclamation.

The hall exploded. People roared, stamped, cheered, clapped, jumped on chairs, waved. Then someone in the audience remembered that Mrs. Stowe was present, and as the word was passed around, all the cheering turned into two words. "Mrs. Stowe!" the audience shouted. "Mrs. Stowe! Mrs. Stowe!" Harriet made her way to the railing of the balcony, looked down at the wildly rejoicing crowd, smiled, and waved. These were her own people, celebrating their mutual triumph. Listening to the deafening recognition she was being given, she knew that this was the moment she had been working toward all through the writing of *Uncle Tom's Cabin,* before the writing, and after. Battles were still to be fought. Some might be lost, some won, but now that the war had been set on the right path, Harriet had confidence that Mr. Lincoln would win it. Having done what she could, she shed her public life as if it were a coat that had served her well but that she no longer needed.

As it happened, just as this chapter of her life was closing, others were closing also. Ten days after the signing of the Proclamation, Lyman Beecher died. He was eighty-seven years old, but that wasn't enough for him. He wished he could have had ten more years.

In addition, the Stowes' life at the Stone Cabin was coming to an end. Calvin had given Andover Seminary notice of his retirement at the end of the school year. What next? For Harriet this meant the chance to build a new house, and she knew exactly where she wanted to build it. She remembered the place on Park River in Hartford that as young girls she and Georgiana May had picked for their dream house. The property was still undeveloped, in the middle of an oak grove, and Harriet bought it. This would be the perfect house, she told Calvin, with all modern conveniences, with decorative features she had seen in some of the most beautiful homes in Europe. She would even outdo Nathaniel Hawthorne, who had written a famous book, *The House of the Seven Gables.* Her house, she reported to a friend, would have *eight* gables. During the spring of 1863 Harriet made plans for the house while Calvin worried about the expense. How could they ever afford the mansion that she had in mind? But Harriet, who had "made do" most of her life with little money, was not going to let money hamper her again. She could always write, couldn't she?

Then suddenly one day in July they stopped thinking about money and houses. In spite of Antietam, the South had continued to win battles, but now at Gettysburg, Pennsylvania, the North won a victory that would turn the tide of the war. At the time, of course, no one could be sure of this, and all Harriet and Calvin could think about was—Fred. He had been with General George Meade's Northern army at Gettysburg. Had he survived? On July 11, a week after the battle, Harriet received word that Fred had been wounded. A fragment of shell had entered his right ear, but he was not in danger.

Calvin left immediately for Gettysburg, but he never got there. Hardly started on his journey, he had his pocket picked in the railroad station at Springfield, Massachusetts, so he turned around and went home. There is no record whether either of the Stowes got to Gettysburg, but in any case they were in close touch with Fred. Charles's son, Fred Beecher, also wounded, was attended in the same hospital by Mrs. Beecher, Charles's wife. By November Fred's ear had still not completely healed, and Harriet arranged for his discharge so she could care for him at home. Unfortunately, it was not his ear that was causing most of his troubles. His drinking problem had worsened. Harriet blamed it on his war injury and did

Harriet Beecher Stowe

everything in her power to cure him, even arranging for long trips at sea, but nothing helped.

In the meantime not all the Beechers had retired to the sidelines of the war. Many Americans worried that England was becoming so impatient with the American war that it might still support the South. Henry Ward Beecher decided to set England right once and for all. In September 1863 he arranged for five speeches to be delivered in five industrial British cities where he expected resentment against the Southern blockade to be strongest. And indeed he did meet hostility. As soon as he started to speak, audiences booed, stamped their feet, and tried to drown him out. They didn't succeed for long. Henry Ward raised his voice, maintained his good humor, and turned on his charm. He was determined to be heard and he was. His speeches made little political difference to England, because by this time it was clear that the North really was winning. But Henry Ward Beecher was impressed with what he had done, and he was the one who reported the details of his tour to the American press. By the time he returned to New York, his tour was described as a "personal triumph" and he had become the man of the hour. A huge meeting was held in New York in his honor, with the mayor acting as host.

And what was Harriet doing besides following the news? She was working on the new house, "busy with drains, sewers, sinks, digging trenches, and above all with manure! You should see the joy," she wrote, "with which I gaze on manure-heaps." Gazing, she would picture a grape arbor and pear trees, "all sorts of roses and posies." Her garden would be an extension of her dream house and actually move into the house wherever possible. She would have a conservatory, vases filled with flowers in every room, and ivy trained to grow around the large windows.

In April 1864 the Stowes moved into Harriet's dream house, which she called Oakholm. The whole family was on hand for the move, although in a few months Charley at fourteen would join the crew of a sailing vessel bound for the Mediterranean. And Georgie, who was being courted by a young minister in Stockbridge, Massachusetts, would soon be planning her wedding. The twins were, as always, their mother's most reliable helpers, and they would continue to be. Elegant-looking as they were, they never married.

The new house turned out, however, to be less of a dream than a nightmare. One thing after another went wrong, as Calvin moaned and groaned about the mounting expense. One night the pipes burst over Calvin's bed. "Oh yes," he shouted. "All the modern conveniences! Shower baths while you sleep!"

As Harriet worked on the house and garden, she went back to writing. She once said, "Writing is my element as swimming is to a duck." And it was a good thing. In order to pay all the bills, she *had* to write. In the spring of 1865 she was especially busy, for Georgie was to be married in June in her mother's dream house whether the roses bloomed on time or not.

But however involved Harriet became in domestic matters, the spring of 1865 became memorable to Harriet and to all Americans for its national news. On April 9 General Robert E. Lee, commander of the Southern army, surrendered to the Northern army at Appomattox Courthouse, Virginia. At last! It was hard to believe—the war was actually *over*. The Union was back together. The slaves were free. By the end of the year

*Harriet's daughters, Eliza Tyler Stowe (left)
and Harriet Beecher Stowe (right)*

slavery would be officially abolished by the Thirteenth Amendment to the Constitution.

But right now was the time for rejoicing. If one Beecher had made "the big war," as Lincoln had told Harriet, another Beecher was to preside over its conclusion. No act was more symbolic of the victory of the Union than the raising of the Stars and Stripes over Fort Sumter, South Carolina. And Henry Ward Beecher was to be the speaker on this occasion. With government representatives and several prominent members of his church, he went from Washington to Charleston, South Carolina, on a federal gunboat. The date was April 14, four years to the day since the United States flag had been lowered. In order to be seen and heard, Henry Ward climbed up on a pile of stones from the ruined fort, and with army and navy men standing at attention, he delivered one of the best speeches of his life. And he, who for so long had found fault with President Lincoln, praised him now for his patience, his fortitude, his wisdom, and his success.

After the ceremony, Henry Ward went to the headquarters of another Beecher to spend the night. James, who had just been made a brevet brigadier general, had come to Charleston to preach to freedmen in the largest church in the city. In uniform as he preached, he placed his sword on the pulpit before him and spoke of peace.

No one could know that on that same evening, while attending the theater, Abraham Lincoln would be shot and killed. Few tragedies in American history have struck the heart as deeply as Lincoln's assassination.

Harriet, who considered Lincoln a friend, had long ago recognized his extraordinary qualities. "He has been a marvel and a phenomenon among statesmen, a new kind of ruler in the earth," she wrote. "There has been something even unearthly about his extreme unselfishness, his utter want of personal ambition, personal self-valuation, personal feeling."

Harriet Beecher Stowe was fifty-four years old, and although she had thirty-one years yet to live, the central drama of her life had been played out. "To think it is all over now, all past," she wrote. "Can anyone realize what a people go through when threatened with the death of their nationality?"

AFTERWORD

Lyman Beecher, born in 1775, a year before the Declaration of Independence was signed, grew up along with his country and believed that the only way to keep the country pure was to reform individuals, one by one. He would make it his business to save souls by holding revivals and striking the fear of God into people. That fear, along with their father's ironclad expectations, hovered over the Beecher children as they were growing up, yet fear alone did not shape them.

Lyman Beecher must have been a powerful, irresistible force in the lives of his children, for his sons, every one of them, with or without some initial defiance, fulfilled his expectations. But once they took command of their own pulpits, it was not fear that these sons passed on, nor was it their father's ruthless, arbitrary God that they commended to their congregations. Their God was a God of love, and though saving souls was part of their ministry, they became social activists. To effect change, they believed, they must enlist in social movements and enter the total life of the community. So the Beecher preachers helped to shape their century, and although they shared common roots, each turned out to be an individualist, often even a rebel.

Thomas K.
Mrs. Hooker   William   Lyman   Edward   Mrs. Perkins Charles   Henry Ward
James   Catharine   Mrs. Stowe

The Beecher family

THE BEECHER SONS

William

William, the oldest, may have been overwhelmed by the very strength of his father's personality. Although he filled the pulpits of a number of small churches, he never developed confidence in himself. Like so many in his family, he had attacks of "hypos," most likely depressions, which were apparently helped by hypnotism, which he himself practiced in turn on others. In his last years, living in Chicago with his daughters, he said, "I don't think God *needs* me. I don't think all I've done or can do amounts to much." He died in 1889, at the age of eighty-seven.

William Beecher

Edward

Like the other Beechers, Edward, the scholar, had trouble accepting his father's strict, uncompromising view of a God who was willing to punish people forever because of that one apple Adam had eaten. At the same time Edward couldn't simply replace his father's God with a more loving, forgiving God without finding a logical way to explain sin. So he invented a complicated theory that he thought would set Christianity on the right path. He believed that people had lived another life before this one. That's when they had sinned and that's what they needed to repent, he said. He wrote a book about his theory, but it was considered too farfetched to be taken seriously. In any case, Edward suffered considerably in his life, not only spiritually but from real hardship. He had six children, including a retarded son, and like so many of his brothers, he was always in need of money.

At eighty-six he fell from a railroad platform in Boston and had a leg crushed by a passing train. With an artificial leg and a cane, he managed well, but again like most of the Beechers, he resented being put on the sidelines, unable to take an active part in life.

Henry Ward

Henry Ward, as the seventh child in his family, claimed that his too-busy father and his too-cold stepmother had never given him the affection or the praise that he craved. He spent his adult life, it seemed, trying to make up for this lack. In the pulpit he not only told his congregation how God loved them, he made them feel that he, Henry Ward Beecher, loved them too. In return he was loved, and the extraordinary success of his ministry sprang from the general aura of love that he created.

Edward Beecher

Henry Ward Beecher

The trouble was that on at least one occasion he may have taken this love too far. In 1870 began what was called the Beecher Scandal, and it was a national one. Henry Ward was accused of adultery, of having an affair with a member of his church, actually with the wife of his best friend. The scandal itself dragged on for years and in 1875 was taken to court. The jury was split in its verdict, so, in effect, Henry Ward was exonerated by default. Although his church not only welcomed him back but paid all his legal expenses as well, his family was torn apart. Harriet, who thought that Henry Ward was perfect, was convinced of his innocence, but Isabella was just as convinced of his guilt. She never stopped trying to persuade him to confess so he could make his peace with God. When at the age of seventy-four (1887) Henry Ward suffered a stroke and was obviously dying, Isabella rushed to his house, hoping he would make a deathbed confession. Eunice, Henry's wife, closed the door in her face.

Charles
After his rebellious interlude in New Orleans, Charles Beecher did, of course, become a preacher but never an orthodox one. Remembering his father's unswerving belief in a God who could condemn even well-meaning people to eternal punishment, Charles wondered if any of the Beecher boys would have gone into the ministry had their father not relied on fear in his teaching. He asked if, as a father himself, he could convert his children without resorting to that fear. Charles was forever raising questions of one kind or another, which made his congregation uneasy. When he admitted to believing in evolution, his church accused him of heresy. He was finally reinstated but largely through the influence of Henry Ward and Harriet.

Charles suffered his share, or even more than his share, of tragedy. His two youngest children, twelve-year-old Hattie and fifteen-year-old Essie, were in a freak boating accident with their twenty-year-old cousin, George (the son of George and Sarah Beecher). All three were drowned. Another drowning in the family! A year later Fred, Charles's son who had stayed in the army after Gettysburg, was killed in a border clash with Indians in Colorado.

In 1870, at the age of fifty-five, Charles, tired of dissensions in the church, moved to Florida, where he worked with freedmen.

Charles Beecher

Thomas

As a young man, before giving in to his father's expectations, Thomas had wanted to be a scientist or an engineer, and throughout his life he would from time to time express his frustration. "I'm sick of this ministerial nonsense," he once exclaimed. On another occasion he wished he could be absorbed in some work "such as the age calls for."

Actually, he put up with little "ministerial nonsense." "The church of one's boyhood," he declared, "cannot be the church of one's manhood." So he went his own way. Not interested in defending church dogma, he preferred simply to help the folks in his town as he imagined Christ might have done. In his forty-six years in Elmira, his congregation increased from 50 members to 700, and although it was obviously time to build a new church, he said a new church didn't matter to him. He could preach in a park or in a hall or from house to house. But when his members voted for a new church, he made sure it was a church that would serve the people in all aspects of their lives. The new building had a gymnasium, a hospital, a stage, parlors, a kitchen, a library, and billiard and pool tables. Thomas called himself "Teacher of the Park Church." The people called him "Father Tom."

Unlike many of the Beechers, he did not rush out to fight for causes. When the right of women to vote became the issue of the day, he did not support it. Like many people in his day, he believed voting would make women more like men, "thin, shrewd, dry, exacting." Perhaps this attitude was merely an indication of the melancholy streak that ran through the family.

"This is a gloomy world," he once wrote in a despairing moment. "I give it up. . . . I will only endeavor to keep from

Thomas Beecher

its evil, bind up its gashes, shine into the darkness, prophesy heaven and wait—wait—wait, singing songs in the night."

James
After the war James had to find his place in civilian life for the first time. It wasn't easy. For ten years he served as minister in churches in New York state, but he must have been impatient with what Thomas called "ministerial nonsense," for then he decided to live as he really wanted to live. He bought a piece of land, one mile square, with a lake, in a remote wooded area of New York. He and Tom had shared many vacations in such wilderness spots in New York, and this was exactly the kind of place where he felt most at home. He and his wife, Frankie, cleared the ground, built a

cottage, and planted vegetables, living a kind of pioneer life that they both loved. Other settlers, though they lived at a distance, asked James to preach to them, and before long he was known as the "hermit preacher." Those who attended his makeshift services admitted he was "queer," but they loved him.

James told Tom once that he suspected that there was a streak of insanity in the three youngest Beechers. Indeed, he may have recognized that for him it was best to live the life of a hermit. Unfortunately, however, Henry Ward persuaded him to go to Brooklyn and work for the poor. He should never have gone. Within a year he was a patient in the insane asylum in Middletown, New York. For four years he was transferred from one institution to another, hating every minute—begging to get out, yet fearful that if he did, "the cloud" might come down on him again. "I want to be in the open air," he cried.

In the fall of 1886 he was released and went to visit Tom. One evening while sitting on the porch with a group of Tom's friends, he excused himself to go into the house. A few minutes later there was a shot. James Beecher had shot himself through the mouth, just as George had done forty-three years before.

THE BEECHER DAUGHTERS

Of all the Beecher sisters, Mary was the only one who stepped into the traditional role assigned to women without challenging it or defending it. The other three sisters—Catharine, Harriet, and Isabella—may have secretly resented the fact that they were excluded from their father's larger expectations just because they were girls. After all, they had inherited their father's drive and had, like their brothers, been instilled with the unrelenting demands of their father's religion, yet there was no possibility of fulfilling their father's ambitions. None of the three actually renounced the feminine ideals they were taught, yet all managed to maneuver within that framework, elevate it, and change some of its boundaries. They

Mary Beecher Perkins

were born reformers living in an age of reform and they were bound to be heard. They were Beechers.

Catharine
Catharine, the oldest of the children, described her father as having "a passionate love of children"—a different picture from the one Henry Ward presented, and indeed she is sup-

Catharine Beecher

posed to have been Lyman's favorite child. Certainly she echoed his values about the role of women being submissive and limited to the domestic arena. She stuck to this position even after woman's rights became a national issue. But within this domestic arena there were untried opportunities. If women were only educated for their profession as wives and mothers and teachers, they would be the world's *true* ministers. Catharine never changed her mind; she believed what she had always believed and spent her life creating in her mind and on the printed page her ideal woman. Although Catharine's ideal woman might operate diplomatically, using only peace and love to attain her goal, Catharine seldom let peace and love get in her way. As long as she lived, Catharine tried to take charge of everything and everybody. When in her last year she finally settled down in Tom's house, she was restless, anxious to be out and doing. "The government of the world will not be going on a whit worse," Harriet told her, "that you are not doing it." Catharine died in 1878 at the age of seventy-eight.

Isabella

Isabella was openly bitter about the way her father had favored the boys. He gave them all a college education, except for William, who refused it, but when it came to the girls—not a word about it! But if once Isabella felt inadequate and sorry for herself, she was a changed woman after the war. She discovered her talents. She found her *cause* in the suffragist movement and was soon drafting bills for the Connecticut legislature, going on speaking tours with Susan B. Anthony, and calling conventions. In time she contended that women were not only equal to men, they were superior to men. They didn't just deserve to vote, the state of the world would be improved if they did vote. "I keep wondering," she said, "how a gentleman can look me in the face and declare that he was born to rule and I to obey." Indeed, she looked forward to a matriarchy in some ideal future when women would *teach* men how to be honorable husbands and fathers.

Isabella became so convinced of her "divine powers" that some in her family thought she was crazy. Of course this made her more shrill than ever. She saw herself as a director in a huge play, and if she needed support in an argument, she called on the voices of the dead. Isabella had taken up spiritualism, a way of talking to the dead through a medium who interpreted rappings that supposedly came in answer to questions. Many people were experimenting with these séances. Harriet had tried it in Italy with Elizabeth Barrett Browning but, though interested, was not convinced. For Isabella, however, these spiritualist sessions confirmed her authority and enlarged her ego. If some of her actions were thought indiscreet and alienated her from her family, she was in the end reunited with them. Isabella, the last of the Beechers, died in 1907, a woman with a fanatic turn of mind but also an acknowledged leader of the women's movement in its early days.

Harriet

When the woman's-rights movement went into full swing after the war, Harriet did not oppose it as Catharine did nor did she become the extremist that Isabella was. She described herself as being "to some extent a woman's rights woman." Certainly she supported a woman's right to an equal education and career opportunities, but even Catharine had advocated this long before the women's movement had come along. She was in favor of political equality and, although Henry Ward was for a while president of one of the branches of the movement, Harriet was no longer interested in taking the front line in fighting for causes. She didn't go along with easy divorce as some of the extremists did, but she had always been concerned about women's status as second-class citizens. On her return from her first trip to Switzerland, she had expressed her admiration for the way the Swiss addressed married couples. Not only did the wife take the husband's last name, but also the husband took the wife's last name, so in their case Calvin would have become Calvin Stowe Beecher.

Harriet took two independent steps in these postwar years that once she would have thought impossible. In the first place, she joined the Episcopal Church. For a long time she had known she wanted to do this, but in deference to her father, she waited until he died. Then she took up public speaking. It was no longer considered a brash thing for women to do, but even so, when a lecture bureau invited her to make a tour, reading from her works, she was hesitant. Still, she accepted and found that once her initial shyness was over, she, like so many of the Beechers, loved to perform. And she was good at it.

Harriet was no longer living in her dream house. After four years of living in a cold, hard-to-heat house and watching the industrial part of the city creep closer and closer, Harriet and Calvin moved to an exclusive section of Hartford, where Isabella and Mary lived. Thomas Beecher's close friends in Elmira, Mark Twain and his wife, would soon move next door. In addition, Harriet bought a house and orange grove in Mandarin, Florida. She hoped that the outdoor life working in an orange grove might put Fred on his feet. It didn't. In the

Rear parlor at Christmas, Stowe House, Hartford, CT

end Fred shipped out for the West Coast via Cape Horn. Once he was in San Francisco he simply disappeared and was never heard from again. As for young Charley, he had gotten the sea out of his system and he too became a minister—the only third-generation Beecher to do so.

Harriet and Calvin loved their Florida house, where they spent their winters, and their Hartford home, where they were close to relatives. One of Harriet's favorite recreations in these years was croquet. Often in the summer she would visit Henry Ward in his country home in Peekskill, New York, and the two of them would play croquet by the hour, sometimes even after dark.

But Harriet didn't stop writing—short pieces and novels. She wrote six novels after the war, but the two most popular were *Oldtown Folks* and *Poganuc People,* set in her favorite old-time New England and drawing upon Calvin's stories of his childhood. Although Harriet herself had been far from carefree and happy in those old times, she had become nostalgic for them.

Uncle Tom's Cabin, however, remained her masterpiece.

Harriet Beecher Stowe

Not only was it a runaway best-seller, it was the most widely read and perhaps widely admired book of its time. That it is not still read with the same enthusiasm today is perhaps not only because tastes in style have changed but also because the book was written with a specific purpose and that purpose has been fulfilled. If her black characters, and Uncle Tom in particular, have been ridiculed as caricatures, it is probably less the fault of Harriet's book than of the many dramatic adaptations over which Harriet had no control. Whereas Harriet meant Uncle Tom to be a Christlike figure modeled on men like Josiah Henson, these theatric productions often stooped to vaudeville techniques and did indeed turn Uncle Tom into a comic character.

Yet in almost any list today of ten books that have changed the world, *Uncle Tom's Cabin* will appear. Harriet Beecher Stowe was a towering figure in her time, and although Lyman Beecher might not have admitted it, she was the best preacher of them all.

NOTES

Page

7. Like many old-time Puritans, Lyman Beecher was a follower of the French Protestant reformer John Calvin. In New England, Congregational churches followed this doctrine; in other places, Presbyterian churches did.

8. In the nineteenth century, "hypochondria" referred specifically to depression.

10. Lyman's second wife was Harriet Porter.

14. The complete title of the book Harriet had to read was *The Analogy of Religion: Natural and Revealed to the Constitution and Course of Nature.*

15. Harriet and Catharine had a contest to see who could paint a snowy owl faster. Harriet won and she hung her picture in her house.

16. By the time Catharine left Hartford, the Hartford Female Seminary was a well-established institution with a fine reputation.

39. Harriet E. Beecher Stowe. The "E" stands for Elizabeth.

54. Daniel Webster thought his compromise was the only way to maintain peace.

56. It is not clear if Harriet ever actually met Josiah Henson, but at some time she read his autobiography, published in 1849.

57. Zachary Taylor's horse was famous in his day for being allowed to graze on the White House lawn.

59. Harriet and Catharine both liked to draw and paint, and both were good at it.

60. Since no one knew when Christ was born, Lyman, like old-time Puritans, thought it was sacrilegious to assign Christ's birth to what had once been a pagan holiday.

72. Jenny Lind, a Swedish singer, was the most famous soprano of her time.

She was called "the Swedish Nightingale" and created a sensation in 1850–52, when she toured America, giving concerts.

75. Harriet's *Key* included sources she had actually used for *Uncle Tom's Cabin* as well as later quotations and stories that proved her thesis.

76. William Lloyd Garrison published a famous abolitionist newspaper, *The Liberator,* from 1831 to 1865. He did not believe in violence, although the language he used in his propaganda was often violent. To protest slavery, he publicly burned the Constitution on July 4, 1854, and opposed the Civil War until Lincoln issued the Emancipation Proclamation.

76. Harriet was actually invited by the *Committee of the Glasgow New Ladies Society* in Scotland, but that invitation led to many others.

82. It was said that Franklin Pierce did as well as he did in college because he sat near Calvin Stowe during exams.

86. The Missouri Compromise of 1820 was an agreement reached between the North and the South to bring the slave states and free states to an equal representation in the Senate. Maine was admitted as a free state, while Missouri was admitted with no restrictions on slavery. The most important part of this compromise, however, was the agreement that no state north of the latitude 36° 30′ (the southern boundary of Missouri) would in the future be admitted as a slave state. The argument over this act threw the North and South against each other. Henry Clay is given much credit for securing the compromise.

110. Charley was a difficult teenager and had a habit of lying, which, of course, worried Harriet and Calvin. They sent him to preparatory schools, but he rebelled and ran away from the last one. He tried to enlist secretly on a ship, but his parents found out and took him home. His "passion" for the sea was so strong, however, Harriet soon let him go. Apparently the sea did for him what schools had been unable to do.

111. Harriet had five new dates inscribed on her slave bracelet, perhaps at the same time.

   Link 4: Emancipation of slaves in the District of Columbia, April 16, 1862.

   Link 5: Emancipation Proclamation, January 1, 1863.

   Link 6: Maryland becomes a free state, October 13, 1864.

   Link 7: Missouri becomes a free state, January 11, 1865.

   Link 8: The Thirteenth Amendment to the Constitution, abolishing slavery, is ratified, January 31, 1865.

After Harriet's death, someone added her birth date (June 14, 1811) and her death (July 1, 1896) on the ninth link. The first three links were inscribed by the British with the dates when they had outlawed slavery. The tenth link was left blank.

112. Brevet brigadier general was a temporary commission. It meant that he did not receive the pay of a brigadier general although he was given the rank.
121. Thomas was a close friend of the Langdon family in Elmira. When Olivia Langdon married Mark Twain, Thomas officiated at the ceremony.
126. Susan B. Anthony was, along with Elizabeth Cady Stanton, the foremost leader of the women's movement.
129. Calvin Stowe died in 1886 and Harriet in 1896.

BIBLIOGRAPHY

PRIMARY SOURCES

The Stowe-Day Library, Hartford, Connecticut.

SECONDARY SOURCES

Adams, John R. *Harriet Beecher Stowe.* New York: Twayne, 1963.

Andrews, Kenneth. *Nook Farm: Mark Twain's Hartford Circle.* Cambridge: Harvard University Press, 1950.

Beecher, Catharine. *Miss Beecher's Housekeeper and Healthkeeper.* New York: Harper, 1873.

————. *Physiology and Calisthenics: For Schools and Families.* New York: Harper, 1856.

Beecher, Catharine (with Harriet Beecher Stowe). *The American Woman's Home.* New York: J. B. Ford, 1869.

Beecher, Charles. *Autobiography, Correspondence of Lyman Beecher, D.D.* 2 vols. New York: Harper, 1866.

————. *Harriet Beecher Stowe in Europe.* Hartford: Stowe-Day Foundation, 1986.

Boswell, George C., ed. *The Litchfield Book of Days.* Litchfield: Shumway, 1899.

Boydston, Jeanne, Mary Kelly, and Anne Margolis. *The Limits of Sisterhood: The Beecher Sisters on Women's Rights and Woman's Sphere.* Chapel Hill: University of North Carolina Press, 1988.

Buell, Lawrence. *New England Literary Culture.* Cambridge: Cambridge University Press, 1986.

Fields, Annie. *Life and Letters of Harriet Beecher Stowe.* Boston: Houghton Mifflin, 1898.

Gilbertson, Catherine. *Harriet Beecher Stowe.* New York: D. Appleton Century, 1937.

Hibben, Paxton. *Henry Ward Beecher: An American Portrait.* New York: Press of the Readers Club, 1942.

Johnston, Joanna. *Runaway to Heaven: The Story of Harriet Beecher Stowe and Her Era.* New York: Doubleday, 1963.

Kirkham, E. Bruce. *Andover, Gettysburg, and Beyond: The Military Career of Frederick William Stowe.* Salem, MA: Essex Institute Historical Collections, vol. 109, no. 1 (January 1973).

———. *The Building of Uncle Tom's Cabin.* Knoxville: University of Tennessee Press, 1977.

———. *The Education of Charles Edward Stowe.* Hartford, CT: The Connecticut Historical Society, vol. 467, no. 2 (April 1981).

Rugoff, Milton. *The Beechers: An American Family in the 19th Century.* New York: Harper & Row, 1981.

Stowe, Charles Edward. *Life and Letters of Harriet Beecher Stowe.* Boston, New York: Houghton Mifflin, 1889.

Stowe, Harriet Beecher. *Dred: A Tale of the Great Dismal Swamp.* Boston: Phillips Sampson, 1856.

———. *The Minister's Wooing.* New York: Derby & Jackson, 1859.

———. *Oldtown Folks.* Boston: Fields, Osgood, 1869.

———. *The Pearl of Orr's Island.* Boston: Ticknor & Fields, 1862.

———. *Poganuc People.* New York: Fords, Howard & Hulbert, 1878.

———. *Uncle Tom's Cabin; or, Life Among the Lowly.* Boston: John P. Jewett, 1852.

Stowe, Lyman Beecher. *Saints, Sinners, and Beechers.* Indianapolis: Bobbs Merrill, 1934.

Wagenknecht, Edward. *Harriet Beecher Stowe: The Known and the Unknown.* New York: Oxford University Press, 1965.

Wilson, Forrest. *Crusader in Crinoline.* Philadelphia: Lippincott, 1941.

INDEX